Dance Me Younger

Published by The Crescendo Group.
Quogue, New York.

This is a work of fiction. Names, characters, places and incidents either are the product of the author's imagination or are used fictitiously.

Available from www.amazon.com and other retailers.

LCCN: 2015960731

ISBN: 0989006131

ISBN: 13:9780989006132

This book is dedicated to:

My mother, Sylvia;
devoted wife, mother, business woman, artist and flirt

and

Jill, Bernice, Naomi, Barbara and Shirley, dear friends
who didn't make it to the next stage of life

and

To my friends who have aged with me. I apologize for
any confidences I have inadvertently revealed. They
were just too juicy not to include.

ITALY
SEPTEMBER

1: "Now," Says My Birthday. "Now, Or It Will Be Too Late."

Momism 1: You are the merchandise. Display it well.

My perfect nose job and I sit on the patio outside La Trattoria al Gatto Nero in Burano. The houses, rinsed in shades of rose, blue, ochre and lime, present a colorful means for fishermen to find their way home in the fog. The vast display of tints makes this island in the Venetian Lagoon seem suspended from reality, which is a good thing, because I am not alone. For the first time in my 30-year marriage—for the first time—I picked up a man.

You may think I'm sitting on years of unhappiness but quite simply, that is not true. I love my husband, Kevin. Really. We've raised two kids and created amazing memories both in and out of the bedroom. Yet I've often wondered, secretly of course, what it would be like to have sex with someone else. Maybe you have, too. Maybe you've also fantasized about your doctor, your boss, an ex-boyfriend, or even your grown son's friend.

Some years these feelings lie dormant, buried beneath our joyful life together. Other times my imagination pushes me to find the courage to embrace something illicit, something to fill in the gap between virginity and marriage. I never do. This year my wish to explore my sensuality seems impossible to control. "Now," says my birthday. "Now, or it will be too late."

So here I sit in Italy sharing a meal with a stranger. He seems relaxed, digging into his risotto with Goby fish while I feel a little awkward. I search my memory for the advice my mother dispensed when I first started dating a lifetime ago. *Susan*, she'd say, *open another button on your blouse, shorten your skirt and put away the book. Don't let anyone know you're smart.*

Okay, it's not your typical motherly advice but it's what I grew up on. Mom was a magnet for men. She loved to draw them into playful conversations, to smile her way into admiration as long as it didn't interfere with family. It was a game she tried to teach me. It never took. I broke out in red blotches when she flicked her blonde hair, stuck out her chest and enjoyed something that happens between certain men and women.

I didn't listen to her back then. I don't know why I open my button today. I don't understand why I allow the black lace of my new La Perla bra to peek out while I tell myself it's okay. Mom wouldn't even lift one eyebrow if she saw me sitting here.

When Mom died, I thought the push-pull we shared would evaporate. I would be free to be my bookish self, to stop having to explain I am not hiding behind the word shy. I just don't enjoy superficial chitchat.

But I missed her. So, long after she passed, I clung to her wisdom, her Momisms that continue to surface. Sometimes I imagine she encourages me to flirt, to be more playful or at least engage people in pleasant discussions. *It's not just the goal,* she'd say.

It's also the process. More often she reminds me to keep grounded, to be good. That's when I appreciate her the most.

I've been on the edge for a while, ready to flip one way or flop the other. I pretend to hear her words as I stare into my new friend's drop-dead, take-my-breath-away eyes.

Stay faithful, Mom says. *Stay married. Stay.*

I need a break from my private thoughts and I want to escape the power of his eyes. I force myself to shift my gaze, to watch the tourists who stroll in front of our table near narrow canals with boats bobbing in murky water. The tourists pass potted crimson geraniums perched on windowsills between dark wooden shutters. I see people walk by purple and white cyclamen nestled in boxes next to doorways. Here I go, rambling on about colors again but that's part of what makes Burano so special.

If I were a painter this would be paradise, except I am not a painter. Nor am I a tourist ready to buy Venetian glass, scarves and post cards from souvenir shops. I am not anything right now and I feel naked without the comfort or respect of a label.

I watch a girl across the canal. She wanders down a passage to pose for a photo beneath laundry flapping on a clothesline attached to windows. The alley is narrow enough for her extended arms to touch the houses on both sides. One house is raspberry, the other gold. On the main street an old woman tats garments in front of her lace store. There is no garbage, no misplaced scraps of paper, nothing out of place— except me.

The environment is a perfect setting for my husband and me to rejuvenate our relationship, but my Kevin has not been here for the past few days. He's a plastic surgeon (yes, he did my nose) and had to stay in New York to cover a scheduled surgical procedure.

I knew this when I booked my ticket. Plastic surgery is planned months in advance. Patients need to stop aspirin and other meds a few weeks prior to surgery. They also need to allow time afterward for bruises to heal before holidays or migrating to Palm Beach or Palm Springs for the winter.

I was the one who decided to start our vacation early—by myself. I checked my husband's calendar and then bought the tickets. I can only imagine how hurt I would be if Kevin did this to me so I wasn't surprised my husband was not happy. Okay, not happy is an understatement. I remember our conversation less than a week ago.

"Susan," Kevin said, with his arms around me, circling me with his love. "Wait just four days so we can go together. It's easy to change a ticket. Let me switch yours for you."

At first I agreed. Our lives usually revolve around his schedule and I have a history of giving in. Maybe that's why he was stunned when a minute later, I changed my mind. I must admit I, too, was a bit astounded. It was almost like watching myself in a movie. I didn't tell him that the thought of being alone in a foreign country without the anchor of business responsibilities or family or friends was too exciting for me to pass up.

"Kev, you hate to shop," I said, flailing around for an acceptable reason to leave before him, to fly to Italy on my own. "I want to go into every store and try on everything. It takes time to find clothes that fit."

My reasoning sounded lame but it was all I could come up with. Even if you don't approve of my flying off like this, if you are a female past fifty I bet

4

you understand what I mean when I complain about my enlarged chest and expanded hips. They grew after menopause, another marker separating me from my youth. In my heightened emotional state I was able to talk myself into believing my upcoming trip and my fading appearance were all connected and my actions made sense.

"Susan," Kevin said, with his arms still around me, still circling me with his love—or was it an effort to control. "You can shop all you want. I promise I'll be extremely patient."

It was a promise he wouldn't be able to keep, the kind of promise that makes each of us smile at the good intentions. This time it made no difference. Something else was pushing me to grab private moments in an unfamiliar place.

For three months I had been moping around the house, trying to shake off a dull dissatisfaction that was starting to seep into our marriage.

"I want to think about my future away from our everyday life," I said. "It's not about us. It's about me."

He looked into my eyes, nodding yes, trying to be supportive. We both knew he was clueless. I tried to explain again.

"Perhaps a new environment will help me create a new version of myself."

"But I like this version," he said, most likely thinking that would solve my problem. His arms were still around me, still circling me with his love—or was he trying to make sure he wouldn't lose me.

"You are so successful, I feel like a parasite."

"It's not a competition," he said. "We're a family. We're on the same team."

I decided to be blunt. "I need some time alone."

Does it matter that I soon found someone else in Italy to talk to? My new friend is tall and smart, a professor of Italian literature at the University of Bologna. He exudes the joy of a man who believes life will be fine. I marvel at his dancer's posture with muscles that bulge out of the short sleeves of his black T-shirt. A black leather jacket balances on the back of his chair. Sunglasses dangle from the neck of his shirt. A pack of Marlboros lies on the table.

It adds up to a not-quite-Euro trash look, a caricature from the movie *Grease* rather than a genuine person, a man in costume copied from an ad for a watch, an exotic fragrance or leather accessory. His full head of black hair matches his dark Roman eyes and reminds me he is young. Very young.

One would not expect a woman of my age to attract or encourage such a man. On the other hand, I too am tall—and thin. I try to avoid carbs and count my Weight Watchers points though I haven't done so well on this plan in Italy.

But let's get honest here. The reason I don't look my 55 years is thanks to my husband's surgical skills. As I mentioned, he did my nose. That was just the first procedure I requested. It was before we were married, so I had to pay for it.

I had a mommy makeover—a tummy tuck, after Sean and then Jennifer were born. It hurt until I healed, but believe me, it was worth it. My breasts have been lifted. Fraxel laser treatments and chemicals made my face refreshed and smooth while removing those nasty brown spots. Deeper lines near my cheeks have been filled with Restylane, a hyaluronic acid gel. Belotero Balance took care of my fine lines and I don't mind Botox paralyzing my forehead and taking away my expressions.

It sounds like a lot but I didn't overdo it. My face doesn't look plastic and I don't have puffed up lips. Please don't hate me for giving in to my vanity. Compared to some other women, my cosmetic work has been mild. And underneath the enhanced façade I am still the same person I've always been.

The bigger question is what did all this work do for me? And why am I off on my own, flirting instead of feeling content with my beautiful life?

Despite what I see in the mirror, men have stopped noticing me. When I walk down Madison Avenue with my son and his girlfriend, more than one guy has bumped into me. I laugh. I say it's no big deal. I lie. Then I watch the man gaze at the beautiful younger woman in six-inch heels or wedges, his head turned so his eyes can follow her until she crosses the street, perhaps to become his fantasy later that evening.

It's no better when I walk by myself. Attempting eye contact and shooting smiles to strangers no longer brings a warm response. Somewhere between my 50th and 55th birthdays I became invisible.

Even when I wear my restaurant shoes, the footwear I save to go from our apartment to a taxi to a restaurant, it's not different. Mom used to love to show off her long legs in high heels. Though my legs are still in good shape, I know sexy shoes do nothing beyond aggravating my bunions. And I am annoyed that I care.

I have so much good fortune in my life you probably wonder why I bother about brief attention from people I don't know. You might accuse me of turning into my mother or criticize me for becoming shallow and craving validation of my worth anywhere I can get it.

I'm not sure why such meaningless overtures make me smile. I think I just miss me, the familiar person I grew up with. I miss the girl who made her parents proud excelling in sports and music. I miss the woman who put in many hours to develop a strong career. Later I balanced hectic workdays with the even more hectic demands of being a mom. The multi dimensions of my loving family and successful work experience gave me what Kevin called my cheery button. I thrived on all the responsibility.

That's all gone now, replaced by dry skin, thinning hair and aching bones. Every day a little bit more of me fades until I hardly recognize myself.

This past year was the worst. Three months ago I was Director of Public Relations at one of the world's top advertising agencies based in Manhattan. I was building our image and writing press releases about our clients' commercials.

One day, after writing about a cola ad, I was asked to draft a release about our merger. I became uneasy as I glossed over the names of friends who were fired because they were part of a surplus of employees when two companies combine into one.

The next day I was sitting with the Head of Human Resources, as useless as outdated yogurt. Most of the time, I don't talk about my early retirement. If I must, I whisper E.R. I pretend mouthing initials for the words will lessen the impact and conquer depression or erase the restless feeling during the empty hours I now live with. Of course, it doesn't help.

What should I do after I wake up? More charity work? Another book club? Bridge? Mahjong? Golf? What about my closet full of designer suits? Should I wear them to the supermarket? I don't know. I don't know. I don't know.

MANHATTAN
THREE MONTHS EARLIER

2: You Are What You Do

Momism 2: It's not fair, but that's how it is. Deal with it.

It's been three months since I left work, but I still can visualize that Friday morning. As usual, Kevin walked me to the door of our Park Avenue apartment near East 80th Street. He gave me a kiss—a real kiss—and adjusted my scarf. It was 8:00 AM. Not 7:59. Not 8:05. Exactly 8:00 AM. Tomas, the doorman, blew his whistle to hail a cab for me just as he has done almost every weekday for the past 25 years.

In nice weather, I sometimes traded my Ferragamo heels for a pair of Nikes and walked 30 blocks to my mid-town office. Then I pretended to balance a mile and a half of exercise with an extra chocolate chip cookie. I tell you this because it sounds nice. To be honest, I usually took a taxi. This had been my routine since I started at the agency.

Naturally there are differences that evolved over time. I have a cell phone and iPad now and two email addresses. Tomas lost his hair and put on more than a few pounds.

My kids grew up and grew away. I miss the camaraderie of the parents as we stood in muddy fields bundled up against the wind and watched soccer games every weekend. I had to be careful that my eyes followed my Sean and not some other fair-haired boy about the same age in the same uniform. When the kids grew older and into other activities, we lost touch with these parents. Our busy lives took over. I guess they were fake friends.

Sean is now in medical school soon to become a nice half-Jewish doctor. I don't think he will go into plastic surgery like his dad. He wants to help people in a more meaningful way. He is the one I call when we can't figure out how to get from Netflix back to our favorite TV programs.

Jennifer, my beautiful Jenny, has her own apartment downtown. Kev and I gave her the down payment. It was a gift, not a loan. We'll do the same for Sean when he's ready. We're the kind of parents who believe we should help our kids.

Perhaps you think we are spoiling them, stopping them from learning the relationship between work and pay and lifestyle. Some of my friends would agree with you. I didn't have such luxury when I was growing up so I am very happy to be able to make my children's lives a little easier. Besides, Jenny has a good job as a marketer and can handle the mortgage.

Did I mention she is waiting for her live-in boyfriend to make the marriage commitment? We are all waiting for him to make the commitment.

For Jenny's sixteenth birthday, I took her to a gynecologist to get a prescription for contraceptive pills. Despite being a virgin until my wedding night, I prepared my teenage daughter to become sexually active in high school! Ever since, I prayed for her marriage.

Only our third child, our Golden Retriever, Max, remains at home. He knows how to roll over, lie down and give a high-five. He is the delight that keeps us from being empty nesters. When he gets a treat, I swear he smiles. But I digress.

That morning, three months ago, I settled in the back of a cab, buckled my seat belt as I've done since Princess Diana had her accident, and allowed the TV in the taxi to intrude on my thoughts. It was a repeat of the *Today* show with Kevin as the guest.

My husband is a favorite among the Manhattan media. Even I believe the press releases I write for him—the promises inherent in a little nip, a bigger tuck, and shots of Botox, fillers or a peel. I've tried them all. This show covered cosmetic procedures for men.

"There's an increase in men taking care of their appearance," Kevin said. "More and more guys are getting facelifts. They are removing back hair with laser treatments or investing in abdominal etching—liposuction for the waist and chest. A few even choose bicep implants."

"Can you give me a statistic here?" Matt said. "What kind of numbers are we talking about?"

"The American Society of Plastic Surgeons claims that in 2014, men accounted for a combination of 1.2 million cosmetic surgical procedures and minimally invasive cosmetic procedures," Kevin said.

He sounded like the expert he is, commanding and self-assured.

"Of course, with females totaling over 13.6 million of these same procedures, women outnumber men by a very wide margin," he said. "Still, that's a substantial group of males and the number is growing."

"What procedures do they want?" Matt said.

"More and more come in to my office for Botox, soft tissue fillers and chemical peels," Kevin said. "Some ask for eyelid surgery—blepharoplasty, more commonly called an eyelift. This procedure reduces bagginess from lower eyelids and removes excess skin from the upper eyelids."

"What about nose jobs?" Matt asked.

"Some men come in for rhinoplasty—surgery to reshape their nose. It will give them a complete new look," Kevin said.

"Why now?" Matt Lauer asked. "What changed?"

"Youth rules. In many professions the juniors are pushing out their older bosses. Mature men want to appear younger as well as more handsome. Medically, results are better than in the past. Look at these examples," Kevin said, as the camera closed in on before and after photos.

"Depending upon what the patient wants, in many cases we can reshape, rearrange or remove problems with incisions hidden in the nose. There is less scarring and it takes less time to heal."

Kevin had my talking points memorized. It was one of his best interviews and I was glad it was being repeated in taxis all across the city.

"It's not just a nose," he said, flashing his best you-can-trust-me smile. "We personalize each procedure to fit the patient's face. And of course, we create a balanced look."

"A blend of art and science," Matt said.

"Exactly," Kevin said.

"Thank you again, Dr. Kendall," Matt said, holding up a recent copy of *New York* magazine with Kev's photo on the cover. "Nice article, by the way. And now to Al and the weather."

The screen switched to an ad for an anti-wrinkle cream as the driver pulled up in front of my office building where a street musician played a saxophone. I dropped a single in his upturned hat on the ground. I figure a dollar a day, five days a week for almost 52 weeks a year for 25 years brings my contribution close to $6,500, all in the memory of my dad who worked his way through college and dental school playing the sax in a small band.

A crew was busy inside the lobby changing the old agency sign, Batten, Grey & Mather to reflect the new name, Highe Advertising. I hardly noticed, busy humming duets I had played as a child, me at the piano, dad on the saxophone.

I paid no attention to the same sign changes in the lobby on the 55th floor. My burgundy red heels clicked on the parquet floor marking the sound of my upbeat internal rhythm until I reached the Oriental rug.

"Good morning Adele," I said, breezing past the receptionist's oversized mahogany desk, shielding my eyes from the sun streaming in through the floor-to-ceiling windows behind her. I still marveled at the view of the East River, still pinched myself to be part of the world of advertising.

"How's your son?" I asked.

"Much better, thanks. I think your mom's chicken soup recipe helped. I made enough to last over a week."

"Glad to hear it," I said, not letting her know I never cook. Why bother when you can get everything around the corner? I belong to that group of women who pretend it's cheaper to eat out or bring in than to buy all the ingredients. Who knew I would need my mother's chicken soup later that day.

Outside my corner office was a plaque, Susan Kendall, Director, Public Relations. Sophie McMullen, my assistant for the past 18 months, sat at her desk in the hall near my door. She was cute—a skinny blonde Midwestern wanna-be-sophisticate thrilled to be part of my team.

I always felt motherly toward my assistants. I helped them develop skills to advance their careers and listened to the details of their lives, careful to give advice only when asked.

Sometimes they asked me to join them and their friends for a drink after work. They pumped me for tidbits of wisdom, as if I had all the answers to their questions. Most often they sought common sense about their love lives rather than about work.

I worried when Sophie went clubbing in New York. With her family far away—and a conviction that everyone is good—I felt she was too trusting. Sometimes I stepped over our work affiliation and asked her to text me when she arrived home late at night. We were both comfortable with this arrangement.

"Good morning," Sophie said. "I can't find any clips on the new cola campaign. Nothing in *Ad Age*. You have a ten o'clock with the creatives to screen a BMW spot and media wants you to sit in on a Revlon focus group. Your lunch with *The New York Times* is confirmed at The Four Seasons and the Operations Committee meeting is cancelled."

"Good job," I said. "Nice earrings. New?"

Sophie smiled, fixed the button-down collar on her pale blue Ralph Lauren blouse and tapped the photo of her latest boyfriend near her computer. I hoped this relationship would last longer than Sophie's previous ones.

"Oh, I forgot, Personnel wants to see you at four," she said. "I'm afraid we're going to fire another group of people."

"Don't worry so much," I said. "It's probably just another detail about the merger."

The next thing I remember it was 4:00 P.M. and I was perched on the edge of an oversized upholstered chair in front of Mary Steward, Head of Human Resources, watching her shuffle papers.

Some people are described as single, or still single. When it came to Mary everyone said, "Never married." She was only 40, plenty of time to connect— if connection was her goal. But there was something tough in the fit of her tight gray suit combined with her salt and pepper hair that was cut in a severe angle, fashionable with an edge. We called her a bitch behind her back, not because she told people they were newly unemployed but because she seemed to enjoy it.

"Are you telling me I'm fired?" I asked, as I shifted my eyes to the skyline visible behind her.

"No, no of course not," she said. "Your performance has been exemplary. It was your placement of financial stories in *The Wall Street Journal* that helped our agency solidify the merger. We all recognize your contributions."

"But I no longer have my job, right?" I fought the tears about to spill down my cheeks and leak inside the collar of my creamy silk shirt. Executive women are not supposed to cry.

I tried to focus on the East River that glistened outside the floor-to-ceiling window behind Mary's desk. It was no use. I glanced at the office buildings towering above the street below. Then I looked at the Statue of Liberty on Liberty Island far to the right in the Upper New York Bay. In my head I hummed, ever so softly, a few bars of Bill Haley and the Comet's 'Rock Around the Clock' to distance myself, to find some control of the situation. I imagined Mary's face smashed by a cream pie. The tears came anyway.

"What you have is an opportunity to retire before you're too old to enjoy it," Mary said, through a mouth full of bleached-white teeth that matched her oversized white-rimmed glasses. "It's the best exit strategy we can offer." Then she smiled. A smile for God's sake!

I sat back, crossed then uncrossed my ankles to stop my leg from shaking. One of my shoes fell off and I had to work hard to wiggle it back on.

Mary handed me some forms to sign. I dug into my handbag to find my wallet then took out my corporate American Express card. My hands wouldn't let go. She waited. After a few silent moments, I pushed it slowly across the desk, just close enough for her to grab it. As fast as a click of my heels, a blink back of tears, a few more bars of 'Rock Around the Clock,' and 25 years—along with my identity—were gone. Work and my life as I knew it were over.

The agony of early retirement had begun. The successful working mother, a role model for so many young women, was suddenly unemployed. What would Kevin say? How could I tell my children?

"Who'll take my place?" I asked. "Who'll head up Corporate Communications?" I needed to know. I wanted to have an enemy to blame, someone more personal.

"Susan, you know we've been bought by Highe Advertising," Mary said, while I watched her place my credit card inside her top drawer. "Their team will take over all the key positions in our company. Who stays, who goes—that's no longer our decision."

"Who got my job?" I asked a little too loudly.

"One of their up and comers. Nowhere near your experience."

"Who? How old?"

"Her name is Emma Bear," Mary said, as she tilted her head and scratched her skin under the hairline over her ear. "She's 32."

"Thirty-two!" I shouldn't have been surprised. I'd watched young people take over lots of key spots in the agency at much lower salaries. I thought about my 25 years of expertise and the numerous other jobs I had turned down to stay loyal.

"For God's sake, she's a novice! Does management know what they're doing?" I asked.

"Susan, Ms. Bear did very well at Bloomingdale's. She earned more than one promotion in a brief time before she shifted to advertising," Mary said. "Don't underestimate her skills due to her age. More important, we've created a very strong retirement package for you."

So there I sat, listening to my financial options and Mary's final farewell.

"Susan, it's because of the merger."

It's not fair, said my mother inside my head. *But that's how it is. Deal with it.*

News of my early retirement reached my staff before me. Sophie and my team delayed the start of their weekend to help get boxes for my stuff. Most files belonged to the company and stayed behind.

As I packed my old photos with Wayne Gretzky, Mickey Mantle and Paula Abdul on the sets of commercial shoots, the advice my mom had dispensed throughout my life bounced into my head. *It's not who you know. It's what you do. Now I don't do anything*, I thought while adding family snapshots, a crystal vase and my ceramic lamp into a carton.

Sophie, along with my assistant for media outreach, my junior speechwriter, the special events planner and the mid-level writer for the newsletter paraded down the hall with me. They stayed close and I thought about *The Music Man* and 76 trombones marching down the street. Only this wasn't a classic film. This was my life.

My team helped me load everything into a taxi. I carried the largest item, the oil painting that had hung over the couch.

"Tell the saxophonist," I said. "Tell him to make friends with Emma Bear."

3: Emma Wants Perfection

Momism 3: If you aren't married by the time you're 22, you're an old maid.

"Mom, I want a different nose," Emma said, as she stared at herself in the white-framed mirror over her IKEA dresser.

For years, whenever she passed her reflection in a window, a glass, any shiny surface, she lifted the tip to see how she looked. If nobody was around she tried this from many angles. With her new job, she had enough money to have it fixed. She was only a "yes" away from going for it.

"Emma, you look fine. You're beautiful," said her mom, Pat, who was visiting from Cleveland to watch her daughter dance at a Saturday night ballroom dance party at the 92nd Street Y.

Pat was as sincere as she was plain. It wasn't that she let her hair go gray. She never thought about it. Her wardrobe was from Target though she could afford Macy's. She preferred to save for more frequent trips to New York to see her daughter.

Pat and Emma often argued. Maybe it was typical mother-daughter annoyances. Maybe it was a reaction to Emma's move to Manhattan. Pat was determined not to fight with Emma on this trip but

Emma's new obsession with her appearance, and with everyone else's appearance, was grating on her nerves.

Pat had raised Emma to be neat but here she was picking up another pair of jeans, another T-shirt strewn on the floor—and it wasn't the first time. What happened to her daughter's Midwestern roots? When did looks become more important than other values?

"You're just saying I look good because you're my mother," Emma said, as she tightened the belt on her Barbie doll waist."

At 5'2" she maintained her body-to-die-for weight by eating small portions of organic foods. She never touched sugar, gluten, meat or dairy—except when she nibbled a chocolate chip cookie and broke her rules to indulge in a burger. Her nutritionist had become a friend and her personal trainer was practically her "in-case-of-emergency" contact.

"If you get any thinner you'll look like an asparagus with arms," Pat said.

"I've been pureeing fruits and walnuts, Mom, and I've cut out anything processed. I feel so healthy. You should try my wheat grass drinks. I mean, they taste better than they look."

Pat scowled then settled on the bed bracing for the next absurdity her daughter would offer. It didn't take more than a few seconds.

"My ass droops. I guess I have to do more Pilates."

"You already work out five times a week. When do you have time for church?"

"I don't do church," Emma said. "You do church."

Pat looked down and shook her head. She loved Emma but not her new lifestyle. She wondered if she still had any influence over her daughter's choices.

Being a mom to a grown child was sometimes just as challenging as caring for a teenager.

Emma gave her mother her most serious expression then moved the conversation back to her appearance. She wanted to show her mom she had done her homework and knew enough about cosmetic options to make the right choice.

"I'm no foreigner to face fashion," she said. "I'm familiar with the differences between Restylane and Juvederm. I want the chemicals my dermatologist injects into my forehead even though they paralyze my muscles. It sounds yucky but they make me look great. The wrinkles starting to emerge around my mouth are the next area I plan to conquer."

Pat felt defeated but she tried again. She shifted from talking about appearances to something more positive and concrete.

"I don't know about any of that stuff. Tell me about your dancing," she said. "I'm so glad to attend the dance party this evening, just to watch, of course."

"Maybe you'll take a spin around the room," Emma said, with a twirl. "Lots of people come alone and most dancers are friendly. They dance with many different people. Mom, I love ballroom. I'm damn good at it—even the lifts in classes. So many of the other students are too afraid to try."

"And?"

"And once a week I volunteer to assist at a dance studio for young teens. It's a special program so those who can't afford the fee can still take lessons. I teach swing."

Emma waited, expecting a compliment or at least a good word. She craved her mom's approval like her sister always seemed to get. But ever since Emma decided to find a job in New York and take a break from the programmed life her parents had envisioned for her, every visit, every phone call, felt like an attempt at a hostile takeover.

"See," Emma said, when her mom remained silent. "I'm not such a superficial person. After the first few lessons these kids get into it. They are so cute. I do it just to be with the kids."

"And?"

"And? And? And nothing. I hate when you do that. I know why you keep pushing. You want to know about my social life. Well I date, okay."

Emma was frustrated. She wanted to think of her parents as her safe haven while the rest of her life was in flux. She worried about her future, about making a mistake. She worried more than her mom did. Why couldn't her mother offer any encouragement? Emma wanted Pat to believe in her, to believe she would find what she was looking for even if it was different from what her mom would choose.

"But you're still single while your younger sister is married," Pat said. "She already has two kids."

"You think that's news? Did you forget I went to her wedding—and the baby christenings? How can you say this to me? Why can't you be positive like other mothers?"

Emma's mom made her anxious and she was already anxious on her own.

"You think I don't worry about finding a man before it's too late to get pregnant. I don't need you to pressure me every time you come to New York. Because of you, I discussed freezing my eggs with my gynecologist. It's depressing."

Pat was surprised by Emma's outburst but it didn't stop her from pushing her message. She felt too strongly to back off now that she had tackled one of their biggest issues.

"And you named your dog Baby and dress her in pink coats with matching boots," Pat said. "Boots for a dog! She's not a baby even if you put bows behind her ears and carry her everywhere you go."

Emma's white Maltese snuggled up to Pat on the bed. Emma picked up her cell phone and took a photo of them.

"I'm going to post this on Facebook," she said. "You look so cute together."

"Oh Emma, you were such a sweetie. New York has changed you," Pat said, visualizing her daughter as a child and as a young teen, full of life, wanting to help people.

"There are times when I don't recognize this new person. Come home, Emma," Pat said. "Come back to Cleveland and be the person we respect and adore."

Pat didn't think her request would be taken seriously but at least she had to try.

"I'm still that person, Mom." Emma said. "If you see some differences it isn't because of New York. It's because of life. Nothing is near what I expected when I started working. I mean it's so much harder to become independent. Sometimes I wish I could just drop in at the house for one of your home cooked meals. But I really want to make it here. It's exciting to have a chance to see foreign films, hear concerts and taste ethnic foods any time, day or night."

"Cleveland has lots of culture," Pat said. "There's the Cleveland Museum of Contemporary Art, the Cleveland Orchestra and the Cleveland opera. We even have the Rock & Roll Hall of Fame and the Pro Football Hall of Fame. You don't need to live in New York to eat sushi or a bagel. You can have just as much excitement in Cleveland and be near your family. Come home. I wouldn't be surprised if the man of your

24

dreams is waiting for you somewhere in our neighborhood."

"Mom, try to hear me this time. My sister is your clone and thrives on the same lifestyle you have. I am different. I love all of you but I don't want to come back. I want New York to be my home."

"Do you think you can do that?" Pat asked.

"Yes, Mom. I can, if I succeed at work. At Bloomingdale's I planned events and saw the latest fashions before they were displayed in the store. I did well and earned two promotions—and I had fun—but the hours were awful. Between work and dance I had no time to go out on dates."

"So you switched to an ad agency. Are you happier? Just a little bit happier?"

"I was until they merged with another agency. Now I have a bigger position. The pay is better so I can join my friends for dinners out and still save some money. Only at this job I have no idea what I'm doing, you know. I mean I'm afraid I'll get fired and then I won't be able to pay my rent. I might HAVE to come home. In the morning I put on my make up and a confident smile. But inside I'm scared all the time."

Now Pat was getting depressed. Maybe she shouldn't have flown to New York for this visit. She wondered if short phone conversations were better for their relationship.

"I wish I could talk to the woman who had my job. She was quite the pro and everyone in the department says she loved to help young people build their careers."

Pat got up, picked up some dirty laundry from the floor and dumped it into a wicker basket near the closet. Emma hated doing laundry because she despised going down to the basement where the washing machine was located. Some day, she imagined, some day she would have a washer and dryer in her home. Right now, she just let her dirty clothes pile up as long as she could.

"They let her go," Pat said, referring to the woman Emma had replaced. "She must have been incompetent."

"No, Mom. They fired her because she was older and earned more than twice as much as I do. They can't say it or they'll get sued."

"You replaced her. You're dreaming if you think she'll help you."

"Without dreams nothing good happens."

"Emma, your nose, your bum and your job are not your problems. You need to settle down. I hit menopause at 40. Grammie too. Stop looking in the mirror or taking selfies and get yourself out there."

Emma picked up Baby and carried her the short distance to her living room. Pat followed and sat on the couch picking dog hairs off the beige linen fabric.

"I am out there," Emma said. "I give my business card to every potential guy I see and I spend hours on Match.com."

"A computer dating service—isn't that dangerous?"

"Oh Mom, first you criticize me for not trying to meet someone, then you get upset when I do. It's the 21st century. Everyone uses computerized dating services. And I'm careful. I arrange to meet new men in a coffee shop. One of my friends is always sitting at the next table, pretending to work on her computer or reading a book on her Kindle. She is always close enough to hear our conversation."

Emma, master of air kisses, bent down to give her mom a skin-to-skin peck on the cheek. She plopped down next to her then clicked another photo on her iphone, this time a selfie of the two of them.

"Besides, a man is not the only answer in life."

"You're nobody without a man." Pat said, as she got up to carry a dirty glass to a sink full of dishes. She put on rubber gloves and washed a week's worth of plates. Emma followed her, happy for the help.

"Emma, you're too fussy," Pat said.

"You were fussy."

"Yes, but I met your dad in high school. It was different then."

Emma was annoyed. She hated when her mother pulled the everything-was-different routine. Feelings weren't different.

"I'm beyond fussy," she said. "My problem is I can't stand any imperfection. Remember the last guy you met? He refused to bleach his teeth. When I told him I wanted a baby—he stopped calling."

"Maybe his wife didn't mind his teeth."

That hurt. Emma didn't date married men. She didn't want to be responsible for wrecking someone else's family. But if a man was separated and almost divorced when they met, she believed it was okay to risk a connection.

"He told me he had decided to leave his wife before we met," Emma said. "He told me he was getting a divorce. He said he was almost unmarried."
She leaned on the wall at the narrow entrance to the galley kitchen watching her mother's brow furrow and mouth turn down.

"Maybe I can find someone for you back home." Pat said. "What are you looking for?"

"It's very simple. I'm searching for a smart, well-established heterosexual man," Emma said, "and," she added with a mischievous smile, "one who gets manicures—and wants a baby—now."

"I'm serious," Pat said.

"Okay, Mom. I can be serious. It's just that it feels like the single guys are all crazy or gay. They want the latest phone, you know, so they wait for the newest version. It's the same when they date women. The guys are afraid to commit because they think they'll find a better girl tomorrow."

Pat was beyond aggravated. For the first time she understood her cousin's frustration when his son left the family hardware store to become an actor while Daddy paid his bills. She thought about her neighbor's son who became a girl and her friend's daughter who had more tattoos than fingers and toes combined.

Did anyone's grown children turn out the way their parents planned? Perhaps she was being too harsh. Pat calmed herself and tried to sympathize with Emma. Maybe by showing her daughter that she felt her pain and dissatisfaction, she could slip in some pragmatic advice.

"Emma, I know things are tough right now, but if you stop dating married men you might connect," Pat said. "Find someone your age. Someone available. Someone to take care of you."

Her words didn't have the agreeable result Pat was seeking.

"Take care of me!" Emma said. "That's so your generation. I can take care of myself. I may want a man but like I said, I don't need one."

Discussions about not having connected permanently with a man cut deep into Emma's fears. She tried to shift such conversations to superficial things. That way, if her mother criticized what she said, it was easier to ignore.

"And I don't understand, you know, why anyone would put up with fixable flaws," Emma said, knowing she was provoking an argument. "I'll never have flapping jowls."

Pat touched the extra skin on her neck with her hand still inside the rubber glove.

"Why would any modern female walk around with sagging breasts? When I was a kid almost everyone wore braces. Nobody thought that was bad. Nobody scorns fake nails or eyelashes. I have hair extensions. All my friends get Botox. Some are CoolSculpting—freezing away their fat cells. Plastic surgery is just the next step on the way to perfection." Pat gave up on being sympathetic.

"You're talking nonsense," she said, feeling a flush coming over her pale skin.

Emma knew she was talking nonsense. When she verbalized it out loud, it sounded awful. At the same time, part of her believed what she was saying. Still, it was easier to absorb her mother's anger and disappointment about cosmetic enhancements than to have her mother zero in on the meaningful parts of her life. Emma stopped her tirade to light a cigarette.

Pat pulled off the gloves, grabbed the cigarette and put it out.

"Cigarettes don't go with wheat grass juice. I need some fresh air." Pat said. "Now that you're such a big earner you can buy your mother a strong cup of coffee."

4: You Are What You Do

Momism 4: You are older. You should know better.

"Susan, you have to stop sending food to Sean," Kevin said, while I packed a box of Hebrew National salami, Oreos, Lorna Doones, granola bars and other snacks. "He's not a kid in camp. He's in medical school with a deli and a pizza place down the block and a really good cafeteria. He won't starve."

"I know. I know," I said, continuing to fill the carton.

"What's that?" Kevin asked pointing to another box stuffed with linens. "Who's that for?"

"Jenny." I said. "They are sheets for her new apartment. I found them in our closet. Never opened."

Kevin put his arms around me.

"Honey, Jen told you she wants to pick out her linens with Adam. You have to let go. Why don't you call the executive network group? You're not the only senior manager on the loose. Try a meeting."

"Sure. Hello. I'm Susan Kendall. I'm 55 and I lost my job."

"I doubt it's like some 12-step program. You haven't *tried* to get a new job."

I shook my head wondering how I could hate someone I love so much. *He's oblivious*, I thought. *This brilliant man doesn't get it.*

"Right," I said. "Corporate America is waiting for me and all the other displaced old lady executives."

Actually, I should give Kevin credit for trying to be supportive. "Sleep late," he said. "Hire a trainer. Take a Global Affairs course at NYU. Enter Scrabble tournaments. Volunteer at The Mount Sinai Hospital. For God's sake, Susan, time is a gift. Use it."

So I did. I signed up for an Italian literature course at NYU mid-town. The first day I tripped over someone's cane, listened to other retiree's tales of arthritis, hip replacements and doctors who no longer take insurance.

Then I scribbled notes about the books we read. The material was interesting, especially a book called *History: A Novel* by Elsa Morante who showed the impact of World War II and political events on ordinary people. All the books were wonderful and I knew I would reread a few.

You are reading great books. I could hear my mom say. *Finally, you are using your brain again. Enjoy the opportunity to expand your knowledge. Now that you are married it is okay to let people know you are smart.*

I forced myself to get deeper into the books. It worked for a while. But there were many hours left in the day so I met a friend downtown at the Whitney Museum of American Art. Seeing the changing New York skyline with a 360-degree view from the seventh floor terrace of the museum was exhilarating. We took a tour of over 200 works from the museum's main collection with pieces by Willem DeKooning, Jackson Pollock, Georgia O'Keeffe and Edward Hopper. We then sampled lunch at the nearby Standard Grill. That covered Monday. It was enjoyable but without a purpose.

On Tuesday I yearned for the excitement I used to feel when I attended a commercial shoot, chatting with the writers and producers, watching the celebrities deliver their lines and later seeing how the segments were put together in the editing room. Instead, I walked up Madison Avenue to my beauty salon.

I usually wear black but that day I had thrown on a pair of blue jeggings and an oversized beige sweater. Everyone else was in black—the colorists, the hair designers and the trainees who held up my hair while the seasoned professional did the cutting and drying. The coat check lady, the cappuccino lady and the other clientele also were in black. Everyone was in black, except me. Many were in black leather. Even in my beauty salon I didn't fit in. And the overpriced experience filled only two hours. Now what?

The next morning I saw a cooking demonstration on TV while on the treadmill. When I worked I never had time to cook. I even thought about using our food pantry to store my shoes but refrained because that isn't the way it's supposed to be.

This was my chance to refocus my creativity into the kitchen. I retrieved the recipe online. I didn't have an open bottle of white wine so I substituted red. I didn't have brown sugar so I substituted Equal. I didn't have shallots so I used garlic. The result was a mess of ingredients held together by wishful thinking.

Everything I did felt phony. Nobody needed me. I was a balloon without air. My brain was no longer the driving force of my day and I lost my cheery button.

Kevin says I have a big depression. We used to do everything together. If we ate salad, I organized and he chopped. Every so often he selected an opera. Other weekends I chose a concert then we listened to the music before we attended the performance. We even made the bed together! We hiked trails in the Berkshires in sunny or drizzly days. It didn't matter as long as we were near each other. Sometimes we read the same book at the same time so we could discuss it. Not anymore.

For the last few weeks, ever since my forced retirement, I felt Kevin's growing annoyance when I didn't want to go to our golf club, attend fundraisers or join him at medical meetings in Grand Cayman Island or The Breakers in Palm Beach.

I used to be his professional equal. But now when friends ask, "How are you? What are you doing?" I am empty with nothing to say. I mumble about a book I'm reading then turn the question back on them. I know I have to recreate myself, but I am stuck without a vision. My perfect life is no longer perfect.

If you can't change something, my mother said, *change your attitude.*

The next morning, I think it was Thursday but I'm not sure because all the weekdays blend together, I walked Kevin to the door of our apartment where he gave me a peck on the cheek. Granted, it was a short walk from the bedroom down the hall to the front door, but at least I was up at 8:00 AM.

After Kevin left for work, I didn't know what to do. Kevin believes in the power of positive appearances, from something as mundane as a pressed shirt to the more serious indulgence of plastic surgery, everything must look right. I was still in sweat pants and bare feet strolling through every room that was silent, empty, cold.

I turned back to our bedroom and wandered into my closet where my clothes are organized by color. Shoes are in their own built-in sections. Handbags are lined up in protective see-through bags. I caressed my

Armani suits wanting to have a reason to wear one, to be in charge of something, anything. 'Rock Around the Clock' blared in my head then shifted to Tina Turner singing 'Proud Mary.'

My feet started to move, then my shoulders and head. I pulled a skirt off the hanger, held it like a partner and danced. I threw the skirt on the floor and grabbed an evening gown. In between beats I put on matching shoes. After a while, I kicked them off and danced barefoot. The music in my head got louder, stronger.

I smiled for the first time that morning, remembering when I had won best dancer in dance classes in what seemed a lifetime ago, when I felt young and optimistic. I danced into a frenzy. This was not ballroom dancing. This was a free-form way of feeling the music. I shook my head until my hair flew up on my cheeks. Soon the joy left and I was moving in a rage. As quickly as it started, the music stopped. It evaporated from my brain.

Still in the closet, I grabbed a pair of my tight jeans and one of Kevin's baggy sweaters and carried them to the center of the bedroom. Instead of getting dressed I plopped on our bed sobbing. Then I imagined my mother tugging at my shoulder.

Up. Get up. Get dressed, she said. *Put on you-never-know-who-you'll-meet make-up and get out. Go somewhere. Anywhere. Get out.*

By now it must have been 8:30. I was way overdue for a strong cup of coffee. In desperation I had created a daily routine—first stop Starbuck's over on Lexington Avenue between 86th and 87th not far from the subway. I could watch the action from a seat in the back of the cafe. Baby strollers, young moms and nannies filled the place. A woman carried a Yorkie in a white outfit and purple bow.

I was getting accustomed to being alone, lingering over coffee, making up stories about guys busy at their computers pretending to work. I could sit in Starbuck's for hours playing a game with myself. If I were to die unless I selected someone to go to bed with, someone at this split second, which guy would I choose? Perhaps I'd pick the man with the beard drinking a latte in the corner or the older man wearing a baseball cap while eating a scone with crumbs resting on his potbelly. I imagined my mom at the next table.

Susan, can't you think of something more productive than sex with a stranger? Mom said. *You're on the verge of cheating. Stay faithful. Stay happy with your Kevin.*

Cheating? I never do anything. Nobody knows what forbidden adventures I create in silence. Much as I consider it, I can't just go up to someone and say, "Hi, I'm an unemployed, unnecessary, aging married woman. Would you like to go to bed with me?" Even if I did throw out such a preposterous invitation, and the man said yes, would I really do it? And if I did, would it solve anything?

5: Hello Can Be Very Complicated

Momism 5: What you see is not always what you get.

Emma wanted her mom to like New York and to like her neighborhood. East 86th Street was so different from the suburban tree-lined street where she grew up in Cleveland. She doubted her mom would be open to appreciate her bustling Yorkville area of working and middle class people. She would give it a try anyway.

Right outside the door to her apartment building she showed her mother she could buy almost anything: bras from Victoria's Secret, books at Barnes & Noble, sweaters at H&M, make-up at Sephora. Her mom wasn't impressed.

It was hard to have a conversation over the sounds of buses, trucks, cars and road workers. They started to shout.

"How do you live with so much garbage," Pat asked as they moved past black plastic bags piled up to their waists on some curbs.

"I don't look at the garbage. I look at the convenience. I can drop in for a quick manicure at that Korean nail salon," she said, pointing to a small storefront. "If I'm hungry I can buy grapes at a fruit stand or I can go off my diet with a red velvet cupcake at Two Little Red Hens or a burger and something fried at Shake Shack."

The smell of Chinese and Japanese foods spilled out to the street and wafted past the newsstand near an entrance to the subway.

"This doesn't smell like fresh air," Pat said.

Emma ignored the comment.

"Look across the street," she said, pointing to Best Buy on the North side of the street. "Customers are mostly men. They're checking out the newest apps. How can I have a serious relationship with a guy who plays video games—fantasy football with fake teams that win fake things?"

Pat tried to watch whether men or women were entering the store. Their unisex outfits, unisex haircuts and similar sneakers sometimes made it hard to tell how many potential customers were men and which ones were women.

"I blame all the moms with sons born between 1970 and 1980," Emma said. "It's their fault the guys are still single and fucked up. Those mothers should be paying for my therapy. It's their fault I can't find a decent guy."

"First it was the guy's fault. Now it's his mother's fault. When do you take responsibility?" Pat asked as they continued up 86th Street.

"It would be nice to find a husband but it's not as important as having a baby. Only you would be upset if it happened out of order or if I pass on the husband and house combo."

"You're darn right I'd be upset. Quit married men. You don't need a clandestine rendezvous or expensive gifts. You know when it comes to important times like Christmas and Thanksgiving husbands stay with their wives. Do you actually think you can pry one loose to have a baby? I don't understand why you find cheating husbands so appealing."

Emma softened. "Mom, I want my own guy. I don't date cheating husbands. But I do go out with those who are already separated. It seems as if only the almost unmarried ones listen to me. They know how to be there 100 percent when we talk."

"Almost unmarried is still married," Pat said, as she opened the door to Panera. After ordering from the overhead menu and filling their large cups, one with green tea and the other with steaming hot coffee, they carried their purchases to a table.

"Look at the nice boy over there," Pat said, selecting a table near the young man. "Maybe you should say hello."

"I can't Mom. And I'm not shy like I was back in eighth grade. It's just that I judge people along with my first hello. Don't you? Strangers shaking hands use their smile time to place each other in boxes: young, gorgeous, let's get together or frumpy, low energy, not to be in my life."

She continued punching out her thoughts without taking a breath while Pat kept shaking her head.

"He never heard of Crest Whitestrips. Her roots are showing. Her nails are chipped. I can evaluate superficial qualities in a few seconds—all before the start of a conversation."

Emma lowered her voice. "Hello can be very complicated," she whispered as if she were sharing a secret new idea. "And by the way, the boy you pointed out needs a haircut and is way too young for me."
Pat struggled. How could she shift her daughter's attitude to a more realistic, mature way of thinking?

"Emma, even if the boy were older and he met your unbelievable criteria for a good appearance, you haven't thought about the more important qualities—

kindness, intelligence, education, respect for family, common interests and values. No matter how complicated you think hello is, hello doesn't get you any of that information. A perfect looking man could be a nightmare inside and vice versa."

Emma shrugged, dismissing the whole conversation and then dug into her oversized handbag to pull out a copy of *New York* magazine with Dr. Kendall's photo on the cover.

"Mom, this time I've done my homework. I researched rhinoplasty on the Web and visited Dr. Foster, Dr. Baker and Dr. Matarasso. I talked to Dr. Rapaport and Dr. Belin. I even explored options in Los Angeles, Miami and cities in South America."

"Are we changing subjects again? I can't keep up with you," Pat said. "If you spent this much time on your job instead of your nose, you might not be worried about getting fired."

"Jesus, why are you getting negative again? Why can't you appreciate how thorough I am?" Emma said, before getting up and ordering another green tea for herself and a decaf coffee with a 470-calorie blueberry muffin for her mother.

"I wish you had been with me when I compared in-office operating rooms. You would get it if you watched computers morph photos of my nose. Dr. Kendall is one of the few top surgeons who use a computer to show patients what they would look like. I'd love you to help me choose the best shape," Emma said with a pout.

"If you change your nose you won't look like me anymore," Pat said softly. "You won't look like you are part of our family. Just be happy with what God gave you."

"Oh, Mommy," Emma said, while giving her mom a big hug. "I never thought of it like that. I'll still have your eyes. I won't look so different. Just better."

"What a waste of money."

"My new secretary, Sophie, was the deciding factor," Emma said. "She hasn't had any plastic surgery but she knows all about Dr. Kendall. She worked for his wife, the lady who had my job. Sophie swears he's the best, or at least he has the best reputation."

"Don't you think that's a bit too close?"

Emma placed her finger on her mouth. "Shh. No negativity," she said. "When I entered his office I knew I had made the right choice."

"You've seen him already! Well at least promise me you'll stop dating married men, I mean soon to be divorced men. It's a pattern that seems to be as hard for you to break as smoking."

"Now who's changing the subject?" Emma said. "First I need to take care of my nose, Mom. Life is good when you take action."

6: Emma Goes To A Dance Party

Momism 6: You can do it if you try.

"I'm just going to watch," Pat said, as Emma grabbed her mom's hand and tried to pull her onto the huge hardwood floor in Buttenwieser Hall. The 92nd Street YM-YWHA was hosting a ballroom dance party and Emma had already changed into her dancing shoes, the ones she had bought at Worldtone Dance over on 8th Avenue and 38th Street. She had splurged on a Freed of London pair with open toes, a strap and the standard suede sole. Pat wore her flats.

"Mom, at least you can take the lesson. I'll be your partner. Not everyone is coupled and sometimes there are more women than men so it isn't unusual for girls to dance together."

Couples were already dancing, circling the perimeter of the room that was 48' by 46'. With two-story high ceilings the place was big enough to host weddings and gala events. It was daunting to Pat.

"Oh, I don't know, honey. I haven't danced since my high school prom. Everyone looks so confident. This isn't for me."

"Mom, you won best dancer in high school. You're the one who always tells me I can do anything if

41

I try. So, like, now I can tell you the same thing. You can do it if you try, right?"

"I do watch *Dancing with the Stars*," Pat said. "At least the men in this room are not wearing their shirts open and showing off waxed chests. People look regular here."

The pre-party lesson was about to begin. Everyone lined up facing the instructor. Other dance teachers mingled in the crowd to correct someone's posture—raise an elbow or a chin. The music was turned off and the instructor demonstrated the steps for a fox trot, first for the men then for the women. He encouraged everyone to try the steps in slow motion. Then he picked up speed, "and five, six seven, eight."

Though Emma was in the midst of the crowd, she watched her mom standing on the sidelines near one of the many card tables and chairs lining the walls. Pat tried to stay unnoticed while she snapped her fingers and moved her shoulders in time to the music.

Most of the participants already knew the steps. Lots of them had been on the social dance circuit for years and knew each other well enough to dance together, though they probably had no social contact outside of the dance party. Some had been on dancing cruises or dancing weekends at hotels. The environment was very welcoming and friendly.

When the lesson was over and the music was turned on, the majority of more than 100 participants coupled off and started to dance counter clockwise around the room. You could tell some dancers were still counting softly to themselves.

Those who already knew the basics branched out to more complicated steps. The music then shifted to a waltz and dancers seemed to float by in graceful harmony. Emma returned to her mom who seemed glued to the floor.

"Okay, Mom. You flew all the way here to watch me dance so I am going to dance. Why don't you sit down while I find a partner. If you change your mind and want to give it a try, wave to me and I'll come right back to dance with you."

Pat felt proud watching Emma dance. She saw the smile on her daughter's face and knew Emma was as happy now as she had been way back in time when she had taken ballet lessons. Though ballroom and ballet were different styles of dance, all the scrimping to pay for those lessons now seemed worth it.

After dancing a Paso Doble, a samba, a quickstep and an Argentine tango, Emma bought two glasses of wine at the cash bar in the nearby lounge then circled back to Pat. It would have been shorter to cut across the floor but that was not the proper way to navigate the dance space.

"Oh My God," Emma said, pointing to the far side of the room directly opposite where they were now sitting. "There's Dr. Kendall. I can't believe he's here. I knew he liked to dance from the photos behind his desk but he's here! Come on," she said, as she pulled her mom's hand again. "I can introduce you."

Dr. Kendall was waltzing, but not with his wife. At the last minute Susan had opted not to join him. Since she lost her job, staying home had become her new norm. At first Kevin stayed home with her. But her lack of participation in most of the activities they used to enjoy together was starting to annoy him. This evening he came by himself.

Emma stood still keeping her eyes on him. She waited until he danced in front of her and then tapped him on his shoulder. He thought someone was cutting in so he stopped dancing and turned to face her.

"Hi Dr. Kendall. Remember me?" she asked in her most perky voice. "I was just in your office. I'm going to be your patient."

Kevin excused himself from his partner and directed his attention to Emma.

"Of course I remember you," he said politely. "It's a good crowd tonight. Everyone is very friendly, swapping partners so the singles are able to dance as much as the couples."

Emma smiled her best bleached-teeth smile then turned toward her mom.

"This is my mother," Emma said. "She came to watch me dance. I'm so glad you're here because she is very worried about my upcoming operation. Maybe you can put her at ease."

Kevin extended his hand to Pat and smiled his bleached-teeth smile.

"It's so nice to meet you," he said. "And I understand your hesitancy about cosmetic surgery. All parents worry about their children no matter how old they are. I know. I am always concerned about my Sean and my Jennifer and they no longer live at home. But an operation carries even more fears, especially an optional procedure. Are there any questions I can answer that will make you feel better?"

Pat felt uncomfortable. Meeting Dr. Kendall made Emma's upcoming operation more real. At a loss for words she nodded no, then lowered her eyes.

"I wasn't sure your daughter had made a final decision to move forward," Dr. Kendall said. "If she is ready for her procedure I assure you there's nothing to be alarmed about. It won't be a complicated reshaping."

Ever the gentleman, Dr. Kendall asked Pat if she'd like to dance.

"Oh, no. Not me," Pat said, looking down at her flat shoes.

"I'll dance," Emma said, as the music shifted to swing.

They danced for a few minutes circling the wooden floor, blending with the other dancers, gliding past the heavy drapes covering the windows and mirrors.

"You're such a good dancer," Emma said, surprised that Dr. Kendall was so proficient.

"Thanks," he said blushing. "But you should see Susan dance. I know the steps and I can do them properly. I finally stopped counting out loud. Susan knows the steps then adds soul, a creative flair that makes the moves all her own. I am in awe every time I watch her. Maybe she'll come next time and you can see what I mean."

Emma nodded as politely as she could. After they had moved around the entire perimeter, Dr. Kendall deposited Emma back with her mother.

7: Emma Wants A Famous Surgeon

Momism 7: What's mine is mine and what's yours is mine too.

Emma walked west on 86th St. from Second Avenue to Park Avenue. It was only three long blocks but the social gap was more like a hike from New York to Los Angeles. Once she reached Park, Emma turned left to make her way a few blocks south down to Dr. Kendall's office.

She was well aware that Park Avenue, from 60th Street to the mid 90's, is its own elite enclave, a quiet residential complex of multi-million dollar apartments each with its own group of uniformed doormen who watch over their residents.

Along the way she passed a dog walker with a dozen dogs and a dozen bags for pooper scooping. She marveled that so many animals didn't get tangled and trip the walker. This day, a set of matching French Bulldogs wore color coordinated dog coats. Emma watched them stop to greet other dog walkers while all the dogs sniffed each other and wagged their tails.

Despite the dogs, the streets she strolled were cleaner than those near her building. There were no sandwich wrappers or stray papers, no water bottles left to roll in the wind.

Emma was a little early so she stopped to gaze up at the windows of some of the older buildings. She wondered what the homes looked like inside. She had heard apartments are decorated, not furnished. Brand new kitchens and bathrooms are redone. Expensive art sits on walls painted white or shades of gray, sky or canary. Rumor has it children on Park Avenue are signed up for private school in utero.

Dr. Kendall was one of those children, a Park Avenue thoroughbred. He grew up on the wide boulevard, raised his kids there and serves on the Board of his building.

The signage on the outside door of his office, just a few blocks north of his apartment, is so discreet Emma had trouble finding it the first time. Today was her second visit so she knew where to go.

She wobbled a little as her stiletto boots sank into the carpet in the waiting room. She tried not to stare at a young girl with puffed lips and a bandage across the bridge of her nose.

I'm not going to do my lips, she thought while deliberately brushing her leg against the leg of a man who was reading, absorbed in a copy of *Men's Health.* She felt herself totter and quickly settled into an empty chair near an older woman whose skin was as clear as her beige silk blouse. *Chemicals,* thought Emma as she fidgeted, skimmed through a magazine then plopped it on the glass coffee table next to a fresh white orchid.

She started to light a cigarette. The receptionist smiled at her with just her mouth. Her dark eyes didn't move. Her brow was solid, her face frozen. She shook her index finger from side to side indicating no smoking allowed.

Emma got up and almost tripped on the man's Italian leather shoes on her way to the door. She wondered if he stuck his foot out on purpose then smiled, realizing he stood up and was following her out.

She put a cigarette in her mouth then fumbled through her handbag in search of a match. He flicked on a lighter in his manicured hand and lit her cigarette, then lit his own that was already dangling from his lips.

They inhaled simultaneously, in perfect rhythm. If you judge a conversation by words, not much happened. If you count a look, a nod and a slow grin, it made sense for them to exchange business cards. She turned and allowed him to watch her backside sway as she ambled back to the waiting room. He trailed a few puffs later but by then, Emma was inside Dr. Kendall's office.

Perhaps it was the doctor's white coat over his shirt and tie or the Queen Anne desk that gave Dr. Kendall his authoritative aura, especially after Emma had seen him in a casual shirt and slacks and dance shoes. The framed magazine articles and degrees from Williams College and Harvard Medical School helped cement his credibility, as did a snapshot of him with Matt Lauer on the *Today* show.

Her plastic surgeon would be the best, even though he was the husband of the woman she had replaced at the ad agency. Awkward? Maybe, but she'd get over it.

The same *New York* magazine Emma had shown her mom rested on Kevin's desk next to a snapshot of Susan and Kevin dancing together.

Okay, you want everyone to know you're a family man, she thought.

"Well Miss Bear. This is your second visit so I assume you have decided to move forward," he said, holding up photos she had taken after her first visit.

"The prints came out well. Look here. You can see your nose from many angles."

Dr. Kendall's style was professional but when Emma looked into his blue eyes she hoped he was attracted to her. Not that she wanted to do anything. Just—well—it would be nice to be noticed.

"How's your mom?" he asked politely.

It wasn't the conversation she wanted but she went with it. She had no choice.

"Thank you for asking. She's fine. I love those dance parties because I get to dance with people from different dance studios. And wow, are you popular! You are so kind to the women who cut in, especially the heavy older lady with the chiffon scarf tied to her wrist. That was some sexy Tango."

"It's the right thing to do," he said.

"You're practically a pro."

"You really have been watching," he said. "Susan and I take lessons—have for years."

"Me too," Emma said in a flat voice. "But the reason I'm here is because after I read about you in *New York* Magazine, Sophie, your wife's secretary, insisted I see you..."

Kevin jerked back. He tapped his desk with his Mont Blanc pen.

"So you're the Emma who got Susan's job," he said slowly, reconsidering whether or not he should accept this girl as a patient.

She nodded. "And everyone still loves her. Of course, I also looked you up online and you know, here I am. I trust you. The other doctors are just names. With you—it's like family."

Kevin rested his chin on his hand then snapped back to a professional posture. He picked up one of Emma's photos. With his pen he pointed to the bump on her nose.

"See this bump right here—it will be softened."

"I'm a little scared," she said.

"That's natural, but I assure you everything will be fine." It was his standard line to build confidence. He shifted the computer screen to face her. "After you're sedated I'll make my incisions and begin to sculpt. See, here, on the computer."

She watched her nose morph into a new nose on the screen.

"Yes," Emma said, with her fists almost in the air, not quite an old cheerleader movement left over from her high school days. Her enthusiasm was out of proportion to the moment.

"Are you okay?" he asked. "It's not exactly something to cheer about. It's a serious operation. Are you sure you're ready for this?"

She moved forward. He leaned away and picked up another photo. Her voice became breathy, like a bad actress trying out for the part of a vamp. He decided to ignore the drama. Maybe she was just nervous.

"I'll shave the cartilage part of the hump then file the bony part," he said. "Every millimeter is important for balance."

"Kevin, you make it sound so easy."

Kevin scowled when she used his first name. If she wasn't being rude, for sure she was being inappropriate. He opened his mouth but said nothing.

"How long will it take?" she asked.

"About an hour. Then you'll be moved to recovery." He stood up. "Come with me. I'll show you our new in-office operating room. It's state of the art and accredited."

As she followed, he continued to talk her through the rest of the procedure.

"We'll reduce the swelling with ice and some herbal supplements. I like Bromelain, an anti-inflammatory enzyme derived from pineapple stems."

"Will it make me smell like tropical fruit?"

Kevin ignored the question. He was beginning to feel uneasy about this patient. He hoped she was stable enough for surgery.

"In just one or two days we'll remove the nose packing and by the end of the week, the splint on the bridge of your nose."

They returned to his office. Still standing, Emma pointed to the abundance of photos lining his shelves behind his desk: his kids at soccer with their dad as coach, Kevin and his Golden Retriever, Kevin holding the hand of his daughter, Jennifer, when she was a little girl, Kevin and Sean running the New York City marathon. In between, she stared at many shots of Susan—dancing, in gym clothes, in a black evening gown. Most prominent was a headshot of Susan smiling. Susan, Susan, Susan.

"Would you do this operation on your wife?" Emma asked. "Is it safe enough for her?"

"As a matter of fact, I did a comparable procedure on Susan when we met. She doesn't mind my talking about it. There have been many medical advances since then. In the end, you'll have a similar softened profile—but one more appropriate for your face, of course."

Emma tugged her skirt up a few inches as she sat down. She picked up one of the photos of Susan on the doctor's desk. The silver frame was heavy and it started to slip from her hand. Kevin grabbed it and placed it further away from her reach.

"Do you think I can talk to her? Not about the operation. About work. I'm afraid I can't live up to her reputation. I'm so jittery. I drop things all the time. I'm scared I'll get fired."

Kevin shook his head no. There were too many coincidences circling this patient. Now she was pushing for a favor involving his wife.

"Well that's quite a change of subject," he said. "Please don't take offense but I prefer to keep my patients and my personal life separate."

"Maybe she wouldn't mind. Can't you at least ask her if she would talk to me?"

"I am sure you can understand that Susan is still wounded. She never expected the agency to let her go."

The minute he said it, he regretted sharing so much information. He sat back.

"I don't think it's the right time," he said, regrouping and sounding polite. "Besides, she will want to know our connection. I'll have to tell her you're a patient, that you are getting plastic surgery."

"I don't care who knows I'm having a nose job. Plastic surgery is almost a badge of honor these days. I'm going back to work as soon as possible, even if my face is still bruised. I have three friends who want to see my results before they choose a doctor."

Kevin ignored the implied promise of a recommendation.

"It seems a bit unconventional, but it's also odd you're the person who landed her job and with all the fine plastic surgeons in Manhattan, you want me to be your doctor. Perhaps you should find another plastic surgeon. There are too many coincidences swirling around me."

"Why don't you let your wife decide?"

"I'm confused," Kevin said. "You want my wife to decide whether or not I should perform your nose reshaping or you want my wife to decide if she will speak with you?"

"I already decided I want you to be my plastic surgeon," Emma said. "Can't you let your wife decide if she'll talk to me?"

"Are you always so determined, Ms. Bear? Maybe at some point I'll let my wife make that choice. Now isn't the right time."

He picked up Emma's last photo. "So, any more questions? About the operation?

"No. I'm in. I mean I'll do this. Nose first, wrinkles around my mouth later."

"There's no rush. Read the materials my assistant will give you—then call my office to schedule your procedure."

His subconscious had already decided he would do the surgery though he had some mixed feelings. Despite her mild drama and inappropriate flirtatious behavior, she appeared vulnerable. She was about the same age as his daughter but seemed much more immature. At least that's how she presented herself. He picked up a business card from the top of his desk and wrote on the back.

"Here are my office and cell numbers. I'm reachable any time but please reserve the cell number for emergencies or immediately after surgery."

Kevin rose to emphasize that the consultation was over. Emma got up but didn't move so he walked to the door and held it open for her.

8: Susan Lives From The Heart

Momism 8: Be Nice.

Our kitchen is so orderly and clean when Kevin cooks he could be in an ad for Viking stainless steel appliances. His pressed white apron is just as spotless. We both like it that way.

"Honey, snap out of it," he said, while slicing onions and garlic with his Japanese chef's knife. "You've moped around long enough. We don't need the money."

I chopped broccoli and zucchini haphazardly. Kevin re-cut my veggies in his surgically precise way then tossed a batch into a pan of sizzling olive oil. A box of Barilla spaghetti and an opened can of San Marzano tomatoes sat near a pot of boiling water.

"We should have ordered in," I said.

"We always order in."

He took a break from cooking and placed my arms around his waist. I pulled away. He poured himself Macallan 12 on the rocks then opened a bottle of red wine for me. The soft gurgling sound of the Chianti filling the glass mixed with arias from Puccini's *Tosca*.

Kevin picked up a book from the pile of travel fiction and non-fiction books and magazines stacked on the corner of the counter: *The Food Lovers Guide to Florence, Access Florence and Venice, 1000 Days in Venice, Under the Tuscan Sun.*

"Now you can read all the books you want, go to museums—spend time with friends," he said. "It'll be fun, a chance to try something new. You can have lunch with Jen."

It was a variation on the 'let's have a positive attitude' theme he had adopted right after I left the ad agency. It was getting stale.

"Jenny lunches with her media contacts and I've spent my entire working life scornful of women who do nothing but meet with friends," I said. "Every morning I wake up and think, what now?" I could hear my voice getting louder. "I'm a work-a-bee. Without my job, I'm living in a fog. I can't talk about it without sounding like a Park Avenue spoiled brat."

Kevin put down the book. He looked so perplexed I wanted to leave the room. I needed to be somewhere else, anywhere else, but I stayed. "You don't *get* it, do you? You're famous. You work for yourself. You'll never have to retire. And stop being so condescending."

"Condescending? I'm trying to be supportive."

"Well aren't you the *nice* one," I said. "I suppose you also want me to feel good about helping your darling Emma Bear."

Kevin sighed.

"Whoa! Wait a minute. She's not my darling. She's a patient who asked for your advice about work. It was your idea to invite her here. I repeat, *your* idea to invite her here before dinner."

He turned away, preferring the calm routine of chopping vegetables to the tension generated by his agitated wife.

"If she upsets you so much why'd you let her come here?" he said, over the sound of the opera.

"Curious. I am damn curious about my enemy."

"I don't believe it," he said. "I think you invited her here because you have compassion."

I kept silent then walked to the dining room to set the table for Kev and me and Jenny who would join us later.

"Actually, I feel sorry for her," Kevin shouted from the kitchen. "She's past 30 and unsettled. She's immature enough to believe a nose job will help her find her soul mate. I tried to tell her surgery will only enhance her appearance but she's off with her own set of thoughts."

Kevin joined me in the dining room.

"I think she's a bit desperate. You know how men flee from those vibes. At her age you were married—to your fabulous husband," he said, with a smile, "and with two adorable kids."

I stopped setting the table then faced Kevin with a fork in my hand.

"She has *my* job at *my* agency, then with all the plastic surgeons in Manhattan she chooses *my* husband. Now *I'm* going to make sure she doesn't get fired. I can't believe I agreed to this. What was I thinking?"

"You were thinking with your heart. It's your mothering instinct. Besides, this Emma situation doesn't have a ton to do with you. She didn't get you fired and *your secretary* convinced her to come to me. Oh, I forgot," he said, changing the subject. "Jen called. She's bringing Adam."

"Again? I hope this is serious," I said. "I worry they might linger on hold too long. If they split she'll soon be at the age where some women panic, just like Emma."

Kevin finished prepping dinner. I added another place setting to the table then walked to the living room. I imagined my mom on the couch, dressed in one of her elegant business suits, thumbing through a *Departures* magazine featuring Italy.

Be nice, she said. *Remember the Italian proverb, 'After the game the king and pawn go back in the same box,'* she said, then poured herself a Macallan 12 on the rocks. *Take the high road. That's what I would do.*

Mom, I thought, *I don't know what that proverb has to do with me. As to the high road, that kid took my job away from me.*

She didn't take your job. She's less expensive, I heard Mom say. *You got screwed in the merger. Happens all the time. Take the high road.*

I knew Mom was right. "Okay, Kev," I yelled, hoping he could hear me in the kitchen. "If it were Jenny I'd want someone to help her. I promised Emma 30 minutes. I can pull that off and get her out of here before the kids come—and I can do it with some sort of professional grace."

Kevin walked into the living room and kissed me on the cheek. He put his arms around me. For ten seconds it felt as if things were back to normal, before early retirement, before the big depression.

"Are you ready for my idea?" Kevin asked.

I tilted my head and waited.

"Let's go to the medical conference in the Cayman Islands. We can use a break."

I didn't respond. How could he be so out of touch?

"It'll do us some good. What do you say?"

"Say? When someone asks me what I do, what'll I say? Do you truly expect me to chitchat with the doctors' wives about their shopping and book clubs? I'd feel even worse with the wives who are working and productive like I used to be. No way. Go without me."

There was my mother again. *Susan this is a mistake, a big one. You've got to keep an eye, and a hand, on what you have.*

I opened the magazine to a photo of Venice and visualized a sudden rush of water splashing my face. I could feel the wind blowing my hair as I pictured us riding in a water taxi.

"Kev, I have a better idea. What about Italy? Just the two of us?" I carried the *Departures* magazine to the kitchen and retrieved the Italian travel books. Just like in a B movie, at that moment the doorman rang us. Emma, my merger enemy and maybe more, was here. I told the doorman to send her up.

Kevin greeted her while I held back, humming 'Rock Around the Clock,' positioning myself on the living room couch, crossing my legs and keeping my favorite dark red shoes on though we weren't going anywhere.

"Emma, come in," I heard him say in his professional doctor's voice. "Susan's in the living room. Would you like a drink? Wine, coke or water?"

I didn't hear any hello kisses, not even air kisses. Score one for Kevin.

"Just a diet Coke, Kevin. Thank you," she said.

I could see their reflection in the mirror on the wall near the door. The mirror gave the illusion that our spacious entrance hall was even bigger than it was. She stood smiling in a mini skirt, stiletto boots and a blouse that bared her midriff, not what I expected for a business meeting. This was a business meeting, right?

A tattoo of a flower climbed from inside the top of her blouse and spilled on to the base of her neck. It was a pretty little add-on to her perfect creamy skin. Though she had a bandage across her nose and the tops of her cheeks were bruised, she was beautiful in an every-middle-aged-woman's-nightmare way. In her arms were a box of cookies and her dog. Our dog, Max, barked and wagged his tail, excited to have company.

Who brings a dog to someone's house? My mother said. *This girl has no boundaries.*

Her dog better not pee on our carpet, I thought as I rushed to Kevin's side and placed a big kiss on his cheek while wrapping my arms around his neck. What would you do? How would you declare absolute possession? She didn't seem to notice my not-quite-appropriate gesture but Kevin sure did.

He twisted his head toward me then rolled his eyes. For months I'd been pushing him away. Now I was clingy. Okay, maybe I was a bit over-the-top, but I didn't care. It wasn't the first time in our marriage my insecurities compelled me to make a "he's mine" statement. Embarrassed, Kevin escaped to the kitchen dragging Max with him.

I faced Emma with an outstretched hand. In my most formal style and with a stiff elbow, I tried to create a physical distance. I think I was hoping to take control, not just of the situation but also of myself.

"Hello," I said, then turned to lead her to the living room before she could respond. I watched Emma focus on our art, the black Steinway piano, the antique furniture, the leather-bound books. She tilted her head, I assumed to try to get a glimpse of our kitchen. I guessed it was bigger than her entire apartment.

"Well, where do we begin?" I asked. "What's bothering you at work?" I hoped my voice was crisp, to the point.

She seems so uncomfortable, I mused while I imagined she dropped dead right there—cause unknown, unimportant. I realize the thought doesn't suit my age—or character. It's a mean girl way of thinking and I was never one of those mean girls but one can't always orchestrate thoughts that pop up on their own.

"Thank you sooo much for seeing me, Mrs. Kendall," Emma said. "It's the first time I've been inside an apartment on Park Avenue. I never imagined the ceilings would be so high—and the rooms so big, so much bigger than my rooms. Do you have a washer and dryer inside your apartment?"

"Do I what?" I asked, puzzled by the question.

"I have to go to the basement to do the laundry in my building," she said. "I dream of having a washer and dryer inside my home some day. Do they allow washing machines inside apartments like this?"

"Well, yes, they do. We have a washer and dryer. It's in a nook in the kitchen."

Emma closed her mouth that had stayed open then settled into the sofa with her dog under her arm, the box of cookies still in one hand and the open can of soda in her other hand.

"When I worked at Bloomingdale's I loved to wander on the furniture floor during some of my breaks. This room is so perfect it resembles a display at the store," she said with a smile. "And I mean that in a good way, for sure. Everything is in its place—even the red throw pillows that add a great bit of splash on your white couch."

I had bought the puffy red pillows to add a touch of color to our monochromatic room and I hoped they whispered a hint of my personality. Even though I enjoyed the compliment, I was surprised that this young woman would mention anything about our decor. Clearly, she was trying to be nice.

"I brought you some chocolate chip cookies," she said, handing me the box. "I made them myself. From scratch. I used my mother's recipe. She's a great baker and when I was growing up I used to help her. One time, when I was about nine, Mom and I baked all afternoon. Then I sold the extras at a fundraiser at school. It was a big success and I did it again every year until I left for college."

I accepted the box but didn't open it. I understood from her non-stop talking that she was nervous. I willed myself to be kind but at the same time I hoped she wouldn't spill her diet Coke on my white furniture. I wished Kevin had offered her club soda.

"When I feel homesick," Emma said, "I bake one of Mom's favorite recipes and my spaceless apartment fills with the aroma of butter and sugar and chocolate. The smell of cookies or brownies or cake makes me feel all cozy and the neighbors sometimes knock on my door to share a taste."

"Thank you for the cookies," I said, then placed the box on the glass coffee table to eat after dinner."

And thank you for seeing me," Emma said. "I was worried you'd blame me for taking your job but it wasn't something I planned. I had nothing to do with what happened."

"I know," I said, feeling her fear under her bravado, the kind of fear I had left behind years ago as I succeeded at the ad agency. Score one point for getting older. She reminded me of the youngest employees at the ad agency the first time they attend a meeting, the ones who tell silly jokes to look smart or cool and are then surprised when nobody laughs.

"All the people I manage have been at the company for a long time," Emma said. "They don't listen to anything I say. I have a title but no authority. It's like you're still in charge and they are on automatic pilot. I want to do well but I'm not sure how."

Baby, her dog, licked my hand. I pulled my fingers away. Just because I love my dog doesn't mean I'll warm up to every other dog.

"Do you like the job?" I asked, pleased to learn my presence was missed.

"I like the paycheck," Emma said. "And I don't know if I can land a different job at the same salary. I don't know what else I can do."

I sure didn't know what I was going to do for the next few years, so I had no idea how I could advise her about any changes she should make. All I could offer was help with her current position.

"I want to work but I also want a balanced life, you know," she said, while patting her dog's head. "I power myself with coffee in the morning. Then I work all day. I'm stressed because I don't know what I'm doing and I worry I'll get fired."

She patted her dog's head faster.

"At seven I race to the gym then swallow a Red Bull and vodka to stay alert in the neighborhood bar where I hope to meet someone. At least I get to spend a little time with my friends even if it is on a bar stool checking out the crowd."

I didn't expect such a personal outburst, especially from someone I didn't know. It sounded awful and I felt sorry for her. I understood why Kevin thought she was a bit desperate. I wondered if my daughter was also on the coffee/Red Bull track.

While I was thinking about Jenny, the dog escaped from under Emma's arm and nestled closer to my lap. I edged away trying to create distance between both Emma and her dog. It was a useless maneuver.

"Of course I need Ambien to fall asleep," Emma said. "And my therapist prescribed antidepressants. I try not to take them together because I know it is dangerous to combine meds."

We're both on antidepressants but she sounds like she's from another planet, I thought as I spotted a tear slipping onto her bruised cheek.

"I was an honors student and a cheerleader, Mrs. Kendall. I don't understand why I'm not married and am having so much trouble settling on a career. I can't figure it out and I'm sorry to be so upset in front of you but my friends are living with boyfriends or they don't care about marriage yet and I met a man I like but he says our relationship is too new to make a big commitment after just a few weeks and my mother doesn't get me."

"Wow," I said, at a loss for words, and I am rarely at a loss for words. So much information spilled out to a complete stranger! At least I learned she liked a man other than my husband and that was good to hear. I hoped this man liked her, too.

Poor kid must be bottled up with nobody to talk to, my mom said in my head. *She probably has nobody who would understand.*

I did my best to console her. Really, I did. I told her to take a breath then strategized a plan of action. I missed work so much I had to refrain from volunteering to draft press releases for her. Since I knew all the people at the agency I helped her evaluate which employees might be convinced to join her unspoken team and which ones to ignore.

We explored ways she might gain credibility with key reporters. I asked about Sophie and the saxophone player. I even gave her a hug—until Baby growled.

It was a start for her and for a fraction of a second, a quick flash, I thought maybe this is the beginning of my letting go, passing the baton, as the cliché goes, and finding some sort of closure.

"Can I tell you a secret, Mrs. Kendall?"

Oh no! No more information, I thought. But I had promised her thirty minutes and I was determined to let her play it out her way.

"I want to be a stay-at-home mom," Emma said. "I want to have babies and take care of them. I used to be ashamed to say this with so many feminists putting down stay-at-home moms. But that's how I feel. I want to bake with my kids like my mom did with me. And I don't want a nanny like I see in the park. I don't get why you enjoyed this job. I think being retired would be so much better than what I'm doing."

With this last outburst, I was sucked in. The merger had derailed both of us. It was probably worse for her without the financial cushion I had with my Kevin. For an instant I thought we could help each other overcome our depressions. I promised to meet her again the following week, perhaps at Starbuck's. On her way out she thanked me with a hug then yelled toward the kitchen, "Bye, Kevin."

That's when my anxiety crashed down upon my kindness. *We're done,* I thought as I slammed the door closed. "Kevin," I muttered. KEVIN! I know a doctor or two who allow patients to call them by their first name but not my formal, well-mannered, waspy husband. Since when did he allow one of his patients to be on a first-name basis?

"Well," Kevin said, joining me at the front door.

"I tried to make it easier for her," I said. "Despite her promotions at Bloomingdale's, I think the poor girl is in way over her head at the ad agency. I doubt she can implement my ideas to get better press results. She lacks passion for the company. Her only hope is that she's cheap—excuse the pun. And, Mr. Supportive, what's this Kevin business? What happened to—Dr. Kendall?" I took the box of cookies into the kitchen and tossed them in the garbage.

9: Susan Fights The Big Depression

Momism 9: Enough already.

Kevin looked striking in his custom-made tux and extra shiny shoes but I insisted he attend the fundraiser alone. I had stopped talking to friends. Movie invitations brought an automatic refusal. My favorite activities were off hours at the gym, reading mysteries and the Italian literature assigned for my class at NYU. I zipped through a book every few days. Sometimes I reread the more complicated ones because I had missed so much due to daydreaming.

"Honey, do you want to walk Max with me?" Kevin asked later in the week.

"Too tired," I said, turning to my crossword puzzle.

"How about going out to dinner when I get back?"

"I ate already," I said, with my pen in my mouth.

Kevin and I always went out of our way to have dinner together. Kevin was disappointed I had cut him out of yet another shared activity but he said nothing to further upset me.

"Then I'll pick up something to eat at Citarella. We're scheduled for a dance lesson Thursday night. Mark your calendar."

"Not yet," I said.

That's a bad decision, Mom yelled. *Go with your husband.* I tuned her out. It was the same response I had given Kev last Thursday. I think he was losing patience. By the following week he stopped asking. I didn't care.

The next night, just as we were about to sit down to dinner, Kevin's cell phone rang. I could see Kev check caller I.D., scowl, look at his watch then sigh before he took the call.

"Hello, Emma," he said. "Are you okay? Is everything okay with your nose?"

I couldn't hear her response but I gathered from my husband's annoyed expression it had nothing to do with her operation. At least he wasn't hiding the conversation.

"Well, I am glad you are fine but in the future, I prefer that you call me at the office. I give this number to patients so they can reach me right after surgery. Since you don't have an emergency I think it's best for you to contact me during working hours," he said, while he held his head. "I'm okay. No, I'm not angry, but please don't call me on this number."

Kevin then exchanged a few pleasant good byes, perhaps to avoid hanging up abruptly.

I was used to patients calling my husband on his cell phone once in awhile. In fact, I admired him for being available. But this felt odd. Kevin obviously did not want to hear from Emma yet he chose to answer the call. He could have let his machine take a message but he opted to speak with her.

I decided not to push it. He wasn't hiding the fact she had called. Was I creating a reason to be afraid when there wasn't one? Were such emotions part of middle age? Even before Emma's operation, Kevin told me he had met her mother at the dance party I had skipped. I was sure he would tell me if there was more to tell or the whole thing would go away.

I went back to reading the *Departures* magazine. I figured if I couldn't alter my mood at least I could shift my environment. My head was off on a traveling track.

Now you're thinking right, my mother said and I smiled.

In the next few days I bought two roundtrip air tickets to Italy, booked hotels in Florence and Venice and organized excursions. Kev loved the idea until he realized I had done the unthinkable. Me, the docile, always-by-my-husband's-side, try-to-give-in-to-avoid-an-argument wife, decided to start our trip to Italy without him. I didn't even discuss it in advance. My flight was scheduled four days ahead of his and took me to Florence. His flight was a non-stop to Venice where we would meet. In less than one week, I was packed and Kevin was driving me to the airport, flying along the highway with the top down.

"Susan, tell me again why you won't wait for me," he said, while tapping the steering wheel of our black Porsche convertible on the way to JFK. "I have one operation scheduled. Then we can go together."

"Kev," I said, snuggling low in my seat to avoid the wind. "I told you already, this is the best thing for me. I can shop in Florence, visit museums and maybe feel renewed. I'll meet you in Venice in only four days.

"I am so worried about you all alone in Italy."

"Come on. My friend Annette took time out for a month in France. Four days is nothing. I've flown solo on business trips. That never bothered you."

"You were not alone. You were meeting other executives in your company. This is different. And you've changed, moping around in a daze most of the time. For three months I've watched you become more and more depressed and I've felt your pain. I don't know what to do to help you."

"You felt my pain. Give me a break. You're too busy with your patients and that Emma girl."

I don't know why I threw Emma's name out. Kevin wasn't avoiding me. He was avoiding her. He was trying to get me to join him in all our normal activities. I was the one pulling back.

"Emma? She called on my cell one time," he said. "What's the big deal? I saw her at a dance party. I danced with her once. Come with me next time and see for yourself. You have no reason to worry," he said. "Her operation is over and she's fine. I just don't like to be rude. I'm not hiding anything. This is nothing. You know you can trust me."

"Yes, and you can trust me in Italy," I said. Then I softened. I was touched by his reluctance to let me go.

"You can't do anything to help me. Just have patience while I figure this out."

"Do you really think being alone in Florence will solve anything?"

"I need time to think," I said.

"About what?"

"Life. My life. What do I do now? I'm not going to sit around for the next twenty years."

"Why can't you think at home?"

"It's not the same. Besides, I intend to check out every boutique along Via Tornabuoni. Maybe this time I'll find something that fits on top. It seems like I lost my job and gained a bigger body."

"I can always do a breast reduction if they bother you," he said.

There he was, out of touch again, trying to be my enabler, always looking for a simple solution to keep things the way they were even though everything had changed. I wondered if he could sense my anger by the staccato tone of my answer. "No. More. Surgery. I have to fix myself."

By then we were at the Delta departures.

"I still can't believe you're getting on this plane. You've never done this to me before," Kevin said.

Kevin had been saying this ever since I made my plans. I wasn't surprised he was stating his frustration again.

"This isn't about you. Don't you get it?" I said. "It's about me. Just me. Three nights and four days until Venice. Like you said about Emma, it's no big deal."

"No big deal! Just about you! Listen to what you're saying. It's a statement about us," Kevin said. "I want my old Susan back. I want *us* back. While you're fixing yourself," he said with one arm around me, "think about fixing our relationship. Think about what I can do to raise your spirits and make us better."

Then he handed me a sheet of paper.

"What's this?" I asked.

"It's a list of places I researched for you to visit in Florence," he said. "I want to make sure you see the important sights."

My eyes must have widened and my mouth opened but I didn't say a word. He wasn't coming with me but he was trying to organize my time.

"That is," he added, "if you want to see them."

I was so annoyed he was pulling the 'I'm your savior' routine again. Then we double-parked. He jumped out and lifted my luggage from the back seat, adjusted the collar on my short black coat, put his hand under my chin and kissed me until a guard waved him on. "I miss you already," he whispered in my ear.

Talk about confusion. I could hardly wait to get away, to be independent, but his commitment and sexy style made the moment romantic. Would I find different romance in Italy? If I did, would I have the courage to accept it? Or should I call it stupidity? Were four days enough? I was glad I had packed new black La Perla lingerie.

Of course, Mom was right there. *Italy without Kevin*, she said. *I feel a hurricane coming.*

10: Emma Wants A Baby

Momism 10: Be careful what you ask for. You just might get it.

Emma wrapped her arms around herself in the Cryo Reproductive Center of New York. Overwhelmed by nausea she covered her mouth with her hand and raced from the waiting room where the slightly older women, single women, women with sterile husbands and lesbian women sat separately.

Their eyes followed her down the yellow hallway to the lavatory. Retching, she dropped to her knees on the cold floor and puked her fears into the toilet bowl, emptying her hesitations with every heave. She knew the others could hear her. She heaved again.

She wondered what kind of men came to drop off semen in exchange for extra cash. Would they appeal to her? Would any be interesting enough to talk to, much less father her child? When the nurse brought her to the doctor she held back a new wave of nausea.

"So Ms. Bear. You want a baby," Dr. Arnold said, while looking directly into her eyes.

"Yes. My mother had early menopause. My grandmother was finished at forty. Gray hair, dry skin, weak bones. I can't wait for, you know, the right guy, if there is such a person. I thought I found him but he left for Italy. On vacation. Without me. Maybe I'm in love by myself."

Dr. Arnold scratched some notes on a yellow pad and then opened his mouth to speak.

Emma interrupted him. "Can you tell me who the men are? I mean, they come in here, you know, and um, uh, masturbate for one hundred dollars."

"Well," said Dr. Arnold. Emma interrupted again.

"It's kind of cold, don't you think?"

Dr. Arnold sat back. "One hundred and fifty dollars. Our donors get one hundred and fifty dollars for their specimens. Some are college students. They all need money."

Emma gagged. "I don't feel so good."

"Perhaps we should reschedule."

Emma was afraid she would never come back if she rescheduled. She wanted all the information she could get before she left.

"No. No. I want to stay now. Do I get to see what the guy looks like? What can I know?"

She took out a pack of cigarettes from her purse but didn't light up.

"You will know quite a bit," Dr. Arnold said. "Some donors allow you to see their baby pictures – sometimes a current one. You'll learn his physical traits, medical history. We screen for infectious diseases, too."

"Including HIV?"

"Of course. And you'll learn about your donor's education, even his SAT scores."

"Wow, that's creepy. Can I pick someone who likes to dance? I love to dance, you know. Can I arrange it so our child will dance?"

"Interests are listed. But are you ready to be a single mom? How will you support your child?"

Emma shrugged. "I earn a good living. Maybe when my boyfriend comes back he'll agree to raise this child with me. If not, I want a baby. Now."

"If you have a boyfriend won't he want to be the father of your baby?"

Emma sighed. She had asked herself the same question. Deep down, she hoped he would want to father her child but it was so soon in their relationship– – and she wasn't sure they would last as a couple. Though they were dating, she wasn't even sure they were a couple.

"You might want to talk to him first," Dr. Arnold said. "And there are other considerations. Do you want a proven donor who already had successful conceptions?"

"Well I guess..."

"Not so fast. That means your baby might have half brothers and sisters. Your child can find them on the donor sibling registry when he or she turns 18. One benefit of finding out is to ensure your baby will be able to avoid falling in love with one of its siblings."

"Oh my God. This sounds more like science fiction than life. I guess I want a new donor, right?"

"It's up to you. You never know if the sperm will take but with a new donor there is no track record so there is more risk. If it doesn't take and you choose to be inseminated again, you'll have to pay again. We usually do a diagnostic fertility evaluation for women approaching 40. But you are young so I am not sure we will use Follistim shots or pills such as Clomid or Femara to stimulate your eggs to be fertile. You can also take folic acid supplements and vitamins E and C."

"I read about all those options on the Internet but when you talk about them it sounds so much worse. I don't feel so good again."

Emma decided to slow down, to research possible side effects and evaluate other options. Should she have her doctor place the sperm into her cervix or directly into her uterus? Would one way be more painful? More expensive? More reliable? Or should she have her eggs taken out, inseminated, then put back in? So many decisions and all she felt was nauseous.

Emma bent her head toward her knees. Still, she stayed, skimming through a book of possible donors, reading each man's family and medical history, favorite movies, hobbies. Did it matter if he liked hiking and kayaking? Were those interests passed on with DNA?

Who is my daddy? Emma imagined her child asking.

Your father is donor #4356.

Do I look like him?

Maybe.

Does he like to read?

He said so in his interview.

Can he play the piano?

I don't think so.

Is he tall or short?

Somewhere in the middle.

Did you love him?

No, Emma would have to say. *I did not love him. I didn't know him. I visited a sperm bank to find the best set of genes. I took many weeks to find someone perfect enough to be your daddy. After searching through hundreds of possibilities the man I selected had my coloring—blue eyes, straight blonde hair, fair skin. He did very well on his SAT test.*

Where is he? Can I meet him?

I don't know where he is but your daddy is an open donor. You can find out all about him when you are an adult. You can meet him once. I have it in writing.

Emma pushed away her imaginary conversation and concentrated on the donor packages. She was allowed to select ethnic background, religion, and blood type. If forced to choose between good looks and brains, she believed a good-looking average child would have an easier life than an unattractive smarter child. The genetic varieties were vast, giving her an enormous influence over the child she would conceive.

Dr. Arnold tapped her shoulder.

"Are you okay? I think we've had more than enough for today. You seem to be in a panic. This decision must be made calmly. You need more time."

"I need a cigarette. That's what I need. Maybe I can find my own sperm. If the guy is married with kids he'll be a proven donor. Right?"

11: Susan Takes Off

Momism 11: It shouldn't be this hard.

By now you must be wondering how I got to Burano with Giorgio. I love telling the beginning of the story. It makes me feel sexy, even wicked because I've always been in good girl groups. Spending days with Giorgio was not a good girl thing to do.

I'm always afraid of losing my luggage if I change planes but there were no non-stop flights from New York to Florence so I opted for a connection in Paris. As tempting as it was to stay there for a day or two, I chose a one-hour and 40-minute layover. I hoped that gave me enough time to stand on line at passport control and take the airport bus to another terminal to catch my flight to Florence.

Kevin thought it would be fine so I took his advice, as usual. Besides, choosing a later connection meant I would land in Italy in the afternoon and would lose half a day of touring.

I didn't know it at the time, but I guess my adventure started at JFK airport when the handsome young man sitting behind me on the plane helped me store my bag in the overhead compartment. *He has the most perfect nose,* I thought. I was too engrossed in my own life to start a conversation despite his cute crooked smile.

As we lifted off the runway I felt free. The next minute I worried that Emma's phone call to Kevin signified something. There was no particular reason for my suspicion. Kevin has always been the steady academic doctor keeping me grounded. I decided to push away any nasty thoughts, to get ready for an "out of the routine of marriage" experience, whatever that meant. Then I flip-flopped and felt lonesome.

Oh grow up, Susan. Enjoy your space for a few days, coaxed my mother. *You chose to go to Italy without Kevin. Now have a good time. Just don't do anything you wouldn't want Kevin to do. No double standard belongs here.*

On my connecting flight, half the people on the plane were Italian. Many were warm and friendly—especially the men—or maybe I was friendlier to them. You know how it is when you take a trip—the excitement, usual defenses down, a nod here, a smile there. Once again, the man who had helped me with my luggage in New York, the one with the cute crooked smile, helped lift my carry-on into the compartment above my seat.

After landing, I spotted him racing off with his duffle bag on his shoulder. I swear he winked at me. I had no idea we would meet again. I just knew I wouldn't be hiding behind any of the books I had stuffed into my bag or downloaded onto my Kindle.

The idea of being by myself for four days with nobody tracking my movements prompted my fantasies to flare up. I noticed men traveling, some alone and others with wives, daughters and friends. What would it be like to go to bed with one of them—perhaps the guy wearing a blazer over tight jeans or maybe the man with a bit of gray in his hair. The smell of espresso, the hum of many languages and the festive atmosphere pulled me out of my funk. I felt so strong I walked faster, as if I had a purpose beyond catching a cab.

Then I got two text messages. One was from Kevin wishing me well. The other was from Jennifer reminding me to send her photos of all the interesting places in and around Florence. So much for nobody tracking my movements.

In the heart of the city, the taxi weaved between motorcycles. Despite their noise, they seemed to come around corners without warning. They made me jump in my seat.

Safely belted in the back I thought about all the times I had stood on the curb in New York City waiting for the red hand signaling don't walk to switch to the white light in the shape of a man letting me know it was okay to step into the street. If there were no cars, Kevin and anyone else waiting with us would cross against the light. I would wait, then scurry to catch up with him on the next block, both of us laughing and sharing a hug of acceptance at our differences.

Passengers in my car often urged me to drive the speed limit, sometimes stomping a foot on an imaginary gas pedal. I am the only person I know who has been pulled off the highway for going too slow. I don't shift gears on my bicycle and refuse to swim in the ocean. And downhill skiing is out of the question.

On this trip I was determined not to be scared to break a few simple rules. Maybe I would try some normal activities even if they carried a little risk.

Still, when those noisy motorcycles chugged next to us, I was aware I had no control over anything. I tried to push away the caution that had been ingrained in my brain since I was a little girl.

I was like a kid, moving my head from one side to the next; looking from bicyclers and tour groups to students posing for selfies and shoppers carrying packages. I watched men walking in tight pants or tighter jeans and women parading with chic hairdos. Everyone was wearing a scarf.

I automatically reached to squeeze Kevin's hand to share my excitement. Of course, he wasn't there. Did I miss him or was it a habit?

The taxi stopped in *Piazza Ognissanti*, the busy square on the right bank of the Arno River. The doorman in front of the Westin Excelsior hotel greeted me. It was enough attention to relieve my anxiety. I gave him a warm hello but before I walked inside I took a photo of the sculpture of Hercules fighting a lion and another of the outside of the Church of S. Salvatore. Jen could decide which photos to keep.

Inside I was drawn to the back of the reception area to view the breathtaking stained glass ceiling. The doorman followed.

"I notice you appreciate our lobby," he said, still holding my luggage. "The hotel was a 12th century mansion once partially owned by Napoleon's sister. Can you imagine the parties and the women in gowns who must have filled this room? Staying here will make you part of history, no?"

Was he paid to say this or was such chitchat the Italian way? I liked it too much to care. I made a mental note to take another photo later.

At the front desk the receptionist told me, "You're in luck, Mrs. Kendall. We can upgrade you to a junior suite at no extra cost."

Great, I thought as I turned toward the elevator. *More space to rattle in.*

Of course, I immediately felt ungrateful and could hear my mother saying, *Change that negative attitude, Susan. You're the one who chose to come here alone. Maybe it's a lucky perk. Maybe Kevin arranged it for you. Either way it deserves a smile.*

The lift was small, as most lifts are in Italy, but there was plenty of room for one. Inside my junior suite I slipped off my shoes and let my newly polished toes sink into the carpet. The king size bed with down blankets and feather pillows for two emphasized Kevin's absence. A dozen long stem red roses bloomed in a crystal vase on the antique dresser. The note said, "I miss you. Enjoy for both of us. *Baci*, Kevin."

I dragged myself onto the balcony to gaze down at the glistening water in the Arno River. The Ponte Vecchio was not far, on my left. The fresh air, the energy of the city below, the vast array of red roof-topped buildings and people kayaking in the river motivated me to move as if I were more awake.

It was getting close to mid morning so I took a fast shower and changed into my favorite black slacks and black sweater. Now I was ready to start day one with a cup of cappuccino in the breakfast room in the lobby—just as I had promised Kevin.

12: Susan Connects With Giorgio

Momism 12: It's fun to flirt.

The breakfast room was elegant in an old-world way, though a little dark with its coffered ceiling. It was rather formal for a bright sunny morning. The place was about to close its morning service and was almost empty. I imagined Mom already settled at a table enjoying the damask tablecloth topped with a tiny vase with three yellow flowers.

Okay Susan, pick one—any one, she said. *Pick a table, order cappuccino and start a to-do list. You have four days and there are so many statues and stores.*

I sat down and placed my thick paperback book, *History: A Novel* on the table, sorry I hadn't downloaded it onto my Kindle.

And put away the book! I heard Mom yell as I snapped a photo of the room for Jennifer.

The itinerary of important places Kevin had listed for me to see was similar to the ones he had done for all our vacations. But I, too, can read the tour books and surf the Internet. For this trip I brought my own ideas. I'd be happy moving in slow motion, viewing a fraction of the city's treasures.

Lost in my plans for long lunches in outdoor *trattorias* sampling *crostini, ribollita* and *pappa al pomodoro*, I didn't pay attention to the young man who scooted in just before the restaurant stopped serving. Though the room was empty he sat down at the next table like a driver in an empty parking lot who lines up next to another car despite a multitude of other spaces.

"*Scusa*," he said, removing his sunglasses and hanging them on the neck of his black T-shirt. His eyes sparkled a friendly hello. "That's quite a book you're reading, all 700 pages."

He spoke in English with a delightful accent. I wondered where he was from.

He snapped his fingers at the waiter, ordered a double espresso in Italian then continued talking to me in English as if we knew each other.

I glanced at him, moved the flowers on my table one inch to the left until they were dead center.

"In Italy we call it *La Storia*," he said. "Lots of people like it. Others find it controversial. What about you? Are you enjoying it?"

"I am. It's compelling. And it's heavy," I said with a smile then thrust out my chin ready to test his authenticity. "I probably should get it on my Kindle but sometimes I enjoy feeling the pages and having a real book in my hand."

I focused on his face and noticed how handsome he was. I wondered why he sat so close to me when the room had so many empty tables. I could understand his interest if I were twenty years younger. Nervous, in a high school sort of way, I reverted to the approach I usually rely upon in male/female conversations, even in middle age. I tried to show this man I was smart.

"It captures the essence of motherhood against a brutal background. Ida, the schoolteacher, was such a simple yet resilient person. She was terrified the authorities would discover her half Jewish background.

Reading about how she protected her two sons during and after WWII was emotionally draining."

"She had to endure so many changes," he said, surveying the whole room with an easy quick look.

He bent his elbow on the table, rested his chin on one of his hands and leaned toward me. I was in awe that he could be so relaxed, so comfortable, so quick to initiate a conversation with a stranger.

"It's Elsa Morante's most famous book," he said, staring at me. At least it felt like a stare.

I sipped air from my empty cup.

"Change is difficult even under the best of circumstances but sometimes it forces people to get stronger," I said. I had no idea where that came from so I had no idea what I would say next. Fortunately, Mr. Handsome saved me.

"Very philosophical," he said, with a laugh and a flick of his wrist to sweep away the comment. "You sound American. Most people outside Italy never heard of this book. How come you're reading it?"

I shifted my legs making sure my shoe didn't fall off and clutched my napkin until my knuckles turned red, then white. I liked his pronunciation, foreign but easy to understand. Okay, I also liked the muscles in his arms. Then I felt silly and way too old to notice.

"It's part of an Italian lit course I took at New York University," I said.

"*Brava*! My name is Giorgio," he said, offering his hand to shake mine. *Piacere*. Pleased to meet you. I'm on holiday," he said, as if it were normal for us to have a personal exchange.

I shook his hand and thought he held mine for an extra moment, a beat longer than I expected. He looked at me with the kind of direct eye contact that says I want you—or was I seeing too much? I blinked, removed my hand and avoided his eyes then turned toward where I imagined my mom was sitting.

You have quite an imagination today, my mother said in my head. *Nothing beyond polite is happening. Calm yourself.*

"And you? What brings you to Italy?" he said.

"I'm on a shopping spree until my husband, Kevin, joins me in Venice."

The waiter brought espresso to Giorgio and cappuccino to me. While he moved his Marlboros to make room for his coffee I checked him out again. This was the man who had helped me on the plane. It felt like running into a neighbor or an old friend. It's the same way at home. You see someone in the gym, week after week without saying hello. Then you meet on a train or in a restaurant and you're old buddies. Why didn't I notice the connection right away?

"You helped me with my luggage, right?"

"I did," he said. "I sat behind you from New York to Paris. I also noticed we took the same flight from Paris to Florence."

"I remember and thank-you for your help," I said. "My bag was way too heavy to be a carry on. I'm Susan. *Piacere.*"

We shook hands again, this time in mock formality. I felt a surge of electricity. His happiness was contagious and I greeted him with a big smile.

"I had a meeting in New York. Now I have a few days off from school," he said.

"What are you studying?"

Giorgio laughed.

"I'm not a student. I'm a professor—at the Universita di Bologna—Italian literature. I saw your book and had to meet you."

He leaned back, relaxed, in control.

"You don't look like a professor."

"You mean no tweed blazer?" he asked pointing to his black leather jacket balanced on the back of his chair.

I nodded and wondered if this man would be talking to me if there were any other single women in the restaurant. Was I getting so much attention because it was me or nobody?

"I'm Italian," he said, as if that explained everything.

"So, what brings a native Italian to a hotel in Florence?" I said.

"Like I said, I live in Bologna so I, too, am a guest in this wonderful city."

"Are you wearing CK One?" I asked.

"*Si.* Too much?"

"No. No it's just that my husband wears it—has for years. It's such a coincidence. It's not a new fragrance."

"I don't believe in coincidences," Giorgio said and pointed to the empty chair opposite me at my table.

"May I?"

"Might as well," I said, with a laugh. It sounded so artificial I was embarrassed and played with my hair. He transferred his cigarettes and jacket from his table to mine while continuing to talk.

"Morante was married to Alberto Moravia. They were both half Jewish," he said, jumping topics.

"Like my children," I said, fingering my wedding band, revealing so much about my life, my family's life, in three short words. I was glad he ignored my comment. Such details weren't meant to be part of a superficial conversation between strangers. Why was I delving in like this? Was he so easy to talk to or was I unable to relish being alone as planned?

"Toward the end of the war Elsa and Alberto fled to safety in a town outside Rome," he said. "That's where they were inspired to write *La Ciociaria.* You probably know the movie, *Two Women,* starring Sophia Loren and Jean-Paul Belmondo.

"You're full of interesting trivia. I should take your course," I said, surprised at Giorgio's command of English and at the intellectual level of our discussion. Then I reminded myself he was a professor. Of course we would have an academic conversation.

"Sometimes a new environment can inspire one to do great things," Giorgio said.

I wasn't sure if he was shifting the topic again or referring to Elsa and Alberto's writings. It didn't matter, so I shrugged. It was one of those all-purpose gestures that carry no meaning.

"Maybe Italy will inspire me. I need a new direction."

"Ah, are you leaving something? Or someone?" he asked.

How intrusive, my mother said. *This guy has balls or maybe you said something to make him feel comfortable crossing a formal boundary or maybe I'm thinking too much.*

I ignored my mother's implied warning though it felt quite strong.

"Perfection," I said, surprised at what popped out of my mouth. "I'm fleeing from perfection—or its illusion. I'm trying to figure out how to be when things are no longer the way they are supposed to be."

"That's too philosophical for me," Giorgio said, while waving both hands. He turned quiet.

I checked my watch. It was close to 11:00 AM and I wanted to hit the stores then view the Basilica de Santa Maria del Fiore before lunch. The silence felt awkward.

"I see you are ready to start your day," Giorgio said. "I grew up here. May I show you my Firenze? It's one of the most wonderful cities in Italy."

"If you grew up here, why aren't you staying with your family?" I asked. I knew it was none of my business but I was curious enough to ask anyway.

"My parents moved and I need to be in Florence for a few days. Not business. My soul needs to be here, to drink in memories along with the art and wine. Again, may I show you my Firenze?"

I thought he sounded pompous—saying my soul needs to be here. Still, I was flattered and stalled for more time to—I don't know why I stalled. I wanted to explore Florence with him but I was afraid. He was so young—and unfamiliar. I felt guilty just having the feeling I wanted to say yes when I had told Kevin I wanted to be alone. I tilted my head and looked at Giorgio.

"Why me?"

"Why not? You're here. I'm here," he said, looking around at the empty room. "We have nothing special to do but enjoy the moment."

"That's a bit over the top," I said with a laugh. "You're joking, right?"

"No. I'm serious."

"How old are you?" I asked feeling more matronly than flirty.

"Thirty-five."

"Thirty-five! I'm old enough to be your mother," I said, though I wasn't as surprised as I pretended.

"You could be my cougar," he said, with such a big grin I knew he didn't mean it.

I shook my head and hands indicating no.

"Relax, I was just teasing," he said. "About the cougar, I mean. I'm here on my own. You're here on your own. Why shouldn't I show a lovely visitor the best we have to offer? Besides, in some cultures I'm considered middle aged."

"Are you married?" I asked. Maybe this time I was crossing a boundary. But what difference would it make? Truly make?

"I have a girlfriend. In New York."

I felt more comfortable hearing he was committed to someone. Touring around an "old" lady was safer for his relationship than picking up an attractive young girl.

"Was that your meeting?" I asked.

"So many questions!" he said, then flipped his wrist to push away an explanation.

"Is that where you learned English? You speak very well."

"Thank you. I studied in school, then lived in New York for a while."

He leaned in again. "We're both free today. Let me show you Florence, yes?"

I turned red and it wasn't a hot flash. I was tempted enough to hesitate, then shook my head no. What would Kevin say? I had told my husband I needed to be alone and here I was, considering having company for the entire day.

"No, kiddo. No can do," I said.

"We can discuss Morante's work and check out sculptures. I'll tell you about the other novels I cover."

I bit my bottom lip, looked directly at him.

"Sounds nice but I can't. I'm serious about my shopping mission."

He stood up, dropped some euro on the table then kissed the back of my hand with feigned drama, a character playing a role.

"Such a pity," he said.

"Are you always so dramatic?"

We both laughed. Then he left.

In the excitement of events I picked up my handbag and spilled the vase of flowers. Water dripped onto my favorite black slacks. I was embarrassed and frustrated. My eyes filled with tears.

The waiter, a silver-haired Rossano Brazzi look-alike in a pressed white jacket, black trousers and a wedding band moved to my side. He grabbed a napkin from one of the tables to mop up my mess. Then he took out a fresh handkerchief from his jacket pocket and handed it to me.

I swear I heard music from 'Three Coins in the Fountain.' I stared at his soap-opera-star face. My eyes cleared, then carried the same come-hither eye contact I thought Giorgio had turned on me. In an emotional flip-flop, I smiled. I watched him replace the flowers in the vase while he returned my smile.

Be careful Susan, my mom said. *You are zigging when you should have zagged.*

13: It's Only Lunch

Momism 13: Lunch leads to dinner.

On my way to the stores on Via de Tornabuoni I spotted a Jean Louis David hair salon and dashed in for a European cut. It sounds like a simple spontaneous decision but for me it was major. I have worn the same hairstyle for twenty years. You'd think a change would involve some thought. I did it fast. I walked in, used my hands to explain what I wanted and came out with a new cut that included bouncing along the street with a bit of a confident swagger.

By the time I entered the Salvadore Ferragamo store I felt as special as the architecture. The shop was in the ancient and magnificent Palazzo Spini Feroni. The doors, the ceilings, the history, the shoes!! It was an OMG moment. I took out my phone and snapped photo after photo for Jen of the surroundings—and the shoes. I had to push myself to leave the women's department to check out the ties. They all seemed perfect and I quickly found one for my Kevin, glad he was so easy to please.

In Prada I touched everything, then tried on a blouse. Too tight in the chest. I bought a handbag and a pair of shoes. I always buy shoes. Black shoes. Brown shoes. Navy shoes. Beige shoes. I don't know what made me have the courage to choose a color—not just any color but fire engine red, much brighter than my burgundy red shoes I wore the day I was pushed into early retirement. These definitely were not a neutral color, especially considering my red hair. The big question was whether I would ever wear them when I got back to the states.

In Armani I tried on black pants. Same story— great in the legs, too tight in the hips. I bought a wallet. There was no way I could justify another pair of shoes.

I weaved in and out of every store, the Energizer Bunny of Italian fashion. In one boutique, outfits were lined up in perfect rows. Kevin would love the precision. The room carried a subtle fragrance most likely from a lit candle. A salesgirl, in a navy suit resembling a flight attendant's outfit, attached herself to me. She held up garments that had been folded meticulously and tried to talk me into bold new patterns. One of her associates joined us.

Always wear solids, Mom said. *Clothes should never detract from your face.*

The sales people were annoying but I couldn't shake them. I explained I prefer to be left alone, like at Saks or Barneys or Bloomingdale's where I admit I often mess up displays and shift items from one area to the next, too much in a rush to return garments to their original places. The staff understood English. They did not understand I wanted to shop on my own. They were there to share their expertise. They couldn't understand why I wouldn't I want their help?

The manager left some Japanese women she was helping to assure me I would get money back at the airport if I filled out Value Added Tax forms. The euro was high, the dollar weak. The tax rebate was all the encouragement I needed, not that Kevin would care how much I spent. Finally, in Max Mara, I found a loose jacket that fit my body and my new look, even though it was my usual black.

I could feel my mom telling me it was okay. *Susan, remember when I taught you how to sew then hoped you'd never have to. This is the same thing,* she said. *We used to shop at Alexander's. You know how to be frugal. You married well. You earned your own money and you received a nice severance package. You can have whatever you want. No guilt here.*

Filled with unexplained vigor I raced across Piazza della Repubblica, turned left for a few blocks, then shifted right to face the Duomo. It was another OMG moment. The majestic church with its famed green, pink and white marble exterior took my breath away. I was overwhelmed, immersed in the beauty, the history and the size of the ancient structure.

Perhaps that's why I didn't notice Giorgio following me from a distance. If I had, maybe I wouldn't have been so friendly when we met in the San Lorenzo market not far from the church.

In the outdoor market I concentrated on products, not people. I felt every scarf, trying on more than I needed for myself, determined to bring home many for presents. I wasn't good at bargaining. If the price was too high, I walked away. That's when the vendors called after me.

"Hey, lady. Where are you from? Are you *Francese? Tedesca? Inglese?*" One selected a gray pashmina scarf, folded it, placed it around my neck then held up a hand mirror. I looked at myself and felt good. Must be the hair, I thought, then returned the scarf and pushed my way through the crowd of shoppers to reach the next stand.

"Hey, lady, come back. You are my first customer today. For you I make a special price," the salesman said. "For you only ten euros. Made in Italy, not China. How many do you want? There is a discount if you buy two, still less if you have cash."

So I learned to negotiate. I figured out if I wanted something, but not too much, I had more power. Walking away, for just a second, was the ultimate bargaining tool. While I paid for a dozen scarves I saw Giorgio at the next stall checking out wallets. He didn't notice me until I touched his shoulder.

"Hi," I said, glad to find someone familiar, someone to break my solitude.

He turned and seemed surprised to see me.

"You changed your hair. *Brava*," he said.

"Thanks. Is this a good place for wallets?"

"Not the best. Not the worst."

"I thought the outdoor markets were strictly for tourists," I said. "What a coincidence finding you here."

"Forget coincidences," he said. "Florence is small. You are bound to bump into everyone you know and I'm sort of a tourist since I'm just visiting."

He stopped shopping to watch me try on some shoulder bags. I smelled the leather, opened the zippers, examined the inside and then put them back.

"Maybe I'll decide after lunch," I said to the salesman. I knew I probably wouldn't return but the vendor seemed so sincere and anxious I felt uncomfortable not buying something.

"I'm starving," I said to Giorgio. "Can you suggest a place for lunch? Something outdoors?"

Sounds like you want him to take you to lunch, my mother said. *What are you up to?*

Once again I ignored her voice in my head. It wasn't my plan when I asked for a suggestion but now I liked the idea of eating together. *It's just lunch,* I thought.

"Gilli's. In Piazza della Reppublica," he said. "They serve lunch but they also have the best chocolates. Great history though it is now very touristy. But as a tourist, you should not miss it. I'll show you where it is."

I had just come from there so I knew the way but hell, might as well walk together. I had second thoughts when he moved his hands into his pockets, like Sean did in eighth grade. It made Giorgio seem even younger than he had appeared earlier. I felt matronly. Before I could change my mind about lunch we were in the middle of a Chinese tour group.

"Should we follow their leader? The one with the umbrella in the air?" I asked.

"I have a better idea," he said, as he put his hand on my shoulder and guided me to the other side of the street and off to the piazza. It felt like we were together.

The open square bustled with disheveled young couples and chunky Americans in sneakers. Some people spoke German. A young man with his face painted white, stood in the center wearing a long white robe, hardly moving, a living piece of art, or something like it. I was glad my Sean was in medical school.

When we reached Gilli's I sat at a table near an outdoor heater. I assumed Giorgio would sit with me. Instead, he eased into a chair at the next table and then snapped his fingers for the waiter. I shook my head and waved him over.

"What took you so long?" he asked.

"Very funny," I said sarcastically, thinking how juvenile he was. "Now, help me order."

"What's in the bags?" he asked.

"Gifts."

I pulled out a blue Ferragamo tie with golf clubs on it. Giorgio felt the silk fabric.

"For me?" He winked.

"Don't be silly. It's for Kevin."

"He must play golf."

"Big time. Belongs to two golf clubs. He's on the Board of one. I play golf, too, but in truth I'm more interested in the outfits."

"I prefer futbal," Giorgio said, while I looked at the menu. It was written in Italian, English, German and other languages.

"I'll have a salad and water with gas," I said, trying to stick to my diet.

"In Italy? You must try pasta—lets share *penne alla Medici*—penne with ham, peas and cream—a half portion for each of us. Then, for your main course, how about *tagliata di manzo alla griglia con rucola e scaglie di pecorino*—slices of grilled beef with arugula and pecorino," Giorgio said. "I'll have *trancio di salmone in crosta di pistachio,* fresh salmon fillet in a crust of pistacios. You can taste both and see which one you like better. And we'll have some wine."

I decided to follow Giorgio's lead, but he had already placed the order for both of us without waiting to see if I agreed.

"Later comes the most important treats," he said. "It is what Gilli's is famous for—espresso and chocolates or cake."

Can you guess what I did? I gave in. No salad this time and I admit it was fantastic to have a glass of Pinot Grigio in the middle of the day, much better than my usual no-fat yogurt and bottled water. I paused to breathe slowly, deliberately looking around. With one sip I could feel the cold wine sliding down my throat, coating me with a taste of bravado I didn't have a minute before.

Suddenly there was an awkward silence again much like the time at breakfast. I can't just sit in silence unless I'm with my Kevin. I get too uncomfortable. Giorgio and I were strangers with nothing but a love of

Italian literature and a day in Florence in common. What could we possibly talk about?

"So, Mr. Professor," I said. "Did you read any books by Primo Levi? Or the great novel, *The Leopard* by Giuseppe di Lampedusa?

My question had nothing to do with the beautiful day or exciting environment or people watching, but it's what popped out of my mouth. I guess it was my turn to sound pompous. Giorgio didn't react in a negative way.

"Of course," he said. *The Leopard* was made into a movie directed by Luchino Vicanti starring Burt Lancaster and Claudia Cardinale. In Italian it was called *Il Gattopardo*. Why do you ask? Are you testing me?"

"No. No," I said. "They were required in my adult Italian Lit course at NYU so I wondered what you thought of them. I liked the books so much I asked Kev to read them."

"And?"

"He had no time." I felt badly implying a criticism of my husband who would have been far more charming and conversational than I was if he were here.

Giorgio inhaled his cigarette then exhaled and turned his face toward the sun.

"You have heard cigarettes can kill, right?" I asked knowing it was none of my business if he smoked or not.

Then I felt badly. This young man was not one of my staff. He was not one of my kids' friends. He was not someone I should be mothering or helping to lead a healthier life. Why couldn't I just keep quiet?

"I like to smoke," he said, offering me a drag like it was a joint. I was irritated and tried to raise my eyebrows but had too much Botox to show any expression. Why did I give a damn if this handsome young man smoked himself to death?

"Did you read *Alibi*?" I asked changing back to a neutral subject.

"Yes, yes, a great mystery about a murder in Venice. I loved the description of the Arsenale and how the author weaved in the aftermath of WWII in Italy," Giorgio said. "I don't teach that one but I enjoyed it. Joseph Kanon also wrote *The Good German*. It was made into a movie with George Clooney."

"I love mysteries. I read all of Donna Leon's books. I suppose they are too light for your class."

"Right," he said. "I skimmed a few but they are not part of my course." He took another puff of his cigarette. "Try one. You might like it," he said, sliding the Marlboros toward me.

"No, thanks," I said, waving smoke away with my hand.

Giorgio breathed in another bit of nicotine, turned his face back toward the sun. I hate smoking so much I couldn't control my thoughts from falling out.

"I know it's none of my business, but three packs a day killed my father. I was 12. He didn't know about the toxic metals, the poisons, the carcinogens even arsenic and pesticides he was inhaling. Look it up on the Web if you don't believe me. I tell every smoker I meet but nobody listens. I don't smoke. Kevin doesn't smoke. Our kids don't smoke. We don't allow cigarettes in our home. Get it?"

"I get it. But this isn't your home," he said, then turned toward me with half a smile to soften his abrupt words.

By now we were both a bit edgy. I knew he was trying to ease the tension with one of his crooked smiles but this time his smile didn't look as cute as I had thought on the plane. In fact, it bordered on a snarl.

"Would you let your children smoke?" I asked. I'm not sure why I asked since I didn't care about his answer. I didn't care if I saw him after lunch. Why was I overstepping polite limits? I usually shy away from confrontations. Why was I pulling him into an argument?

"I don't have kids," he said.

"What about your girlfriend? Does she want children?" This was another feeble attempt to change the subject but I probably hit another touchy area. It was not my most tactful day, yet I couldn't stop. Maybe the glass of Pinot Grigio had erased my control button.

Never force anything, my mother said. *Remember, you can't control another person. Do you actually think this young man will listen to you? Do you care if he does?*

"So many personal questions. Does this mean we're friends?" Giorgio asked.

"It means I'm curious. I'm sorry if I stepped over a line," I said. "You don't have to answer."

His body language changed into a more relaxed posture, more amused than serious with our discussion.

"Kids? Yesterday. My girlfriend wants them yesterday. So many girls panic when they reach their thirties. They pressure their boyfriends to move forward before they are ready. My girlfriend threatened to visit a sperm bank when I told her I was going to Italy without her. Can you imagine that?"

"Well, it is rather extreme, like a temper tantrum. Why didn't you bring her here with you? You should be sitting here with her instead of a woman 20 years older. My son would probably say you have a commitment problem."

Giorgio flicked his wrist again as if to erase all details. "Later," he said, and then lit another cigarette while I blew the smoke away and shook my head.

"Why aren't you sitting here with your husband?" he asked.

"Touché," I said, taking another sip of wine and picking at the pasta the waiter had placed before me. "I lost my job—and with it my identity. I thought I needed time alone to figure out what I can do with the rest of my life. How's that for a big answer?"

"Whew!" he said laughing. "It's way too big for me. I can hardly figure out what I should do today or tomorrow or where to go for dinner tonight. I can't imagine the burden you carry trying to plan the rest of your life. You leave no room for spontaneity."

"Everyone needs a plan. If you don't have a plan how can you accomplish your goals?" I asked.

"So let me understand this. You think a few days on your own in Florence will give you answers to plan the rest of your life. If that works, we should start a tour group for all the people who face choices and must start over."

I knew he had a point but I was still in an argumentative mood.

"If you had a plan you would commit to your girlfriend," I said defensively. "Or set her free. You need to think about the future, too."

I couldn't believe I said this. I would never talk this aggressively in a similar situation back home. I wouldn't even talk this way to my kids. What was I doing?

"I do think about my future," he said, "and she is part of it. But it's not so simple. There are complications. Believe me, I'm working on it." He inhaled again.

"If we hang out another minute you have to stop smoking near me so I don't have to breathe in the smoke."

"Okay. I'll stop near you. You sure are stubborn," he said. "At least you're consistent."

"Ouch. That wasn't nice," I said.

I've always been stubborn and I'm surprised it didn't take long for Giorgio to notice.

"Just do me a favor," I said. "Keep the smoke away from me."

"You've got a deal. Do you and Kevin argue like this?" he asked.

"Are you changing the subject again? Since you asked, no, my Kevin and I don't argue. Well, at least not often. Usually I give in though sometimes, over certain topics, as you've just witnessed, I can be very strong-willed," I said grabbing at my wine and taking a sip. Then I finished the rest with one giant gulp.

I stood to snap a picture of the Piazza della Repubblica making sure to capture the carousel in the far corner. Then I shot the outside of Gilli's with their delicate chocolates and sumptuous cakes in the window. Satisfied with my photos, I emailed them to Jen. It was just the break I needed. Thinking about my daughter made me feel happy and connected to my life in New York.

"Name one," he said, when I sat down again. He started to light up another cigarette then put it away.

"One what?" I asked sidetracked by my own thoughts.

"One topic you and Kevin argue about. Maybe I'll learn something for my relationship with my girlfriend. Like what topics to avoid."

I had to give the man credit for listening. And hanging in there for no apparent reason. The only certain thing about this lunch was that neither one of us had to be there. Something must have been acting as the glue. I couldn't figure it out and was puzzled.

"I am strong about religious things," I said, in answer to Giorgio's question. "Kevin wanted a Christmas tree. I didn't."

"I don't understand. A tree is so beautiful."

"Yes, but I didn't want to confuse the kids. I am Jewish. Kevin is Presbyterian. We were happy ignoring our differences before the kids were born. Later we argued. Our parents took sides. Finally, we agreed not to bring Sean and Jen up with either religion. We agreed to let them choose their beliefs when they got older, beyond their teens."

"Now they are older. What did they choose?"

"Nothing. Neither one has any religious beliefs. I celebrate the major Jewish holidays at Park Avenue Synagogue on East 87th Street. Kevin goes to The Brick Presbyterian Church on Park Avenue and 91st Street with his parents. Our kids do nothing. Maybe we made a mistake. What about you? What religion do you want your kids to follow?"

"I haven't thought about it. I'm going to buy some chocolates for us and then we are off to see the sights," he said, getting up and changing the subject."

I was glad the frictional conversations were over. To keep things smooth, and because I wanted to taste the famous sweets, I ignored my diet again.

"Wait," I said, after he returned with a bag of nougat and marzipan and chocolate truffles. "I want to go to La Rinascente. The department store is right here. I can see the entrance."

"Tomorrow," he said picking up my bags. "I can't carry more packages. Right now we are going to see my favorite city starting with Michelangelo's David and ending with a drink in Fiesole overlooking the city before we succumb to jet lag."

14: I'll Never See Him Again

Momism 14: You are somebody's wife.

On day two Giorgio immediately joined me at my table for breakfast. I was glad to see him. On some level I expected to see him. I was even grateful for his company. We had stopped our silly arguments and following our afternoon of touring, I felt comfortable hanging out together. When he dangled the promise of a surprise if I joined him for dinner, I was happy to accept his invitation. I didn't even need the enticement of a surprise.

I prefer not to dine alone. I don't like to walk into a restaurant filled with couples or groups of friends. I don't like to be escorted by the maître d' to a table for two then watch while the waiter removes the second place setting. Saying yes was easy. Besides, now that we weren't verbally entangled in nonsense, Giorgio was delightful.

The only guilt I felt was not mentioning my new friend to Kevin when he called. I shared all the details of the day except my companion. I'm not sure why I left out Giorgio. Nothing was happening sexually and many times I missed my husband. Maybe I was worried Kevin might get jealous because my supposed alone time wasn't as alone as I had planned.

"So lovely lady, Giorgio said, "What will we do today?"

I was pleased at his assumption to spend the day together but I had already made other plans.

"Today I am taking a morning bus tour to Lucca, home of Puccini, because I love his operas—you know—La Boheme, Tosca and Madame Butterfly. I'll be back in the late afternoon."

"Would you like me to join you?" he said. "Or should we meet here at 8:30 for dinner?"

I was conflicted but since I would be with other people on the tour, I didn't need his companionship. Dinner, however, was another situation and I was happy to have company for the evening meal. We agreed to meet in the hotel lobby at 8:30.

After Giorgio left the breakfast room, I grabbed my phone to email Kev and knocked over the flowers again. The same waiter, Roberto was standing by my side with a napkin in one hand and another fresh handkerchief in the other.

Roberto smiled. "Your friend, he makes you nervous?"

"No. I'm just a *klutz*."

"Your hair, *signora*. Very beautiful."

"Thank you," I said, startled that he noticed the change. "They got it right even though I don't speak Italian."

His eyes pulled me into a conversation and I understood the cliché about Italians knowing how to make a woman feel sexy. I loved how I felt. I loved Italy. I loved all Italians and I especially loved Italian men. That said, it was important to me to let Roberto know I was married.

"I'm a little melancholy," I said. "I'm glad to be here but I miss my husband."

"Ah, I understand. I, too, am married. *Sono felice.* I am happy, happy at home but sometimes it is good to, how shall I say, have time alone."

"Would you go on vacation without your wife?"

What's wrong with you? My mother asked. *Why are you getting into such a conversation with someone you don't know? If you must talk to him, talk about the food he serves or why he has so many handkerchiefs.*

"I love my wife," the waiter said. "I'll always be there for her. But sometimes something separate also is very good."

"Separate? Do you mean by yourself or with someone else?"

"I mean with someone else, *signora.* Someone who doesn't know you very well."

"Please don't call me *signora.* It sounds like *madam* and that sounds old. Call me Susan."

Roberto bowed. "*Susanna. Sono Roberto.* I am Roberto. *Piacere.*"

I loved his accent. It was much thicker than Giorgio's and I had to listen carefully to understand what Roberto was saying.

"*Piacere.* Thanks for your handkerchiefs. I don't always spill things and I don't always cry. I'm a bit unnerved. I lost my job—no identity." I couldn't believe I said that.

"No identity? I don't understand. Maybe it's the language or maybe it's an American thing." He looked around to make sure nobody was watching us then moved a stray hair out of my eyes. "Or maybe you are the one who doesn't understand."

I was being absurd so, of course, in my head, Mom appeared next to Roberto. *Susan, leave this guy alone. You'll find your identity without the waiter.*

"You are beautiful, full of life," he said. "Is that not enough? At my age I think it is important to enjoy every moment, every experience life offers. Don't you agree, Susanna?"

I never watch soap operas. How could I listen to such garbage? Chemistry, that's how. I was so attracted to him I played with my hair like I did in high school. I wondered what it would be like to dance with him, to have him put his arm around me and for me to rest my head on his shoulder. I blushed. Then I remembered I am a practical, goal-oriented person who thrives when things are happening the way they are supposed to happen. I had to break from this drivel.

"I think you are full of psychobabble," I said. I smiled to soften my insult. In truth, I wanted to hear so much more.

"Perhaps you can meet me when I finish work" he said, ignoring my comment. "*Alle diciotto in punto*—18:00 sharp, or six o'clock American time. Here."

What a bold leap, I thought, terrified.

"Just for a drink," I heard myself say. "I'm meeting Giorgio for dinner."

This pushed Mom hard.

Stop it. Stop it. STOP IT! Drinks with a waiter. Dinner with a younger man. You are crossing a line. With strangers! Stop. It. Now!

Oh please, I thought. *What difference does it make? I'll never see either one of them again.*

By six o'clock I was wearing my new bright red shoes and walking along the Arno River with Roberto. Our arms were linked as if we were an affectionate old married couple. Our steps were in sync at a leisurely pace while we talked, talked and talked, though I am not sure we understood each other. I told him about my family and how much I loved my Kevin. Roberto vowed he loved his wife. We were equal, vested in our lives back home, stepping out for just a little while.

I smiled when Roberto expressed a desire to be with me. I nodded yes, as if I agreed with him. What I meant was yes, I hear you.

Not once did I look at my feet. My sigh let out all my anxieties and depressed feelings that had been building for the past three months. I didn't think about my identity or my lost job or what I would do tomorrow. It seemed so natural to lean against this man's comfortable soft body. His hand moved from my hair to my perfect nose job and chin, lifting my face.

This is beyond flirting, said my mother. *You're past menopause. You are somebody's wife. This is not for you! Stop it.*

But I didn't stop. Of course, I felt guilty. *It's not instead of Kevin,* I thought. It's extra. One has nothing to do with the other, or am I thinking like a man who wants to cheat?

It was as if I were watching someone else's life. I imagined this total stranger understood me, which was odd because I didn't understand myself. In an instant he had touched something simmering inside, something that had fueled my fantasies for years. Was it curiosity about being with someone new? Was I just flattered to be visible again? Was it a physical desire? Certainly Giorgio's youth and tighter build held the promise of more energy and excitement. But Giorgio was like a friendly puppy. He wasn't coming on to me. Besides, his age made me feel wrinkled, tired, and ancient.

It was Roberto who stirred my body. For the first time in 30 years, I was ready to give in to a side I wasn't sure I had. I was so frightened my leg shook. Then I thought of Diane Lane enjoying *Tuscany Under The Sun.* I thought of Marlena DiBlasi, the author of *1000 Days in Venice,* finding her stranger with the blueberry eyes. It was my turn, my story, my movie.

We heard music drifting down from an apartment above. Roberto put out his hand inviting me to dance. We swayed more than danced, nothing like I learned in ballroom classes and nothing like Kevin and I can do. This was just an excuse for two people to press their bodies together like at a high school prom. To any passersby we appeared to be lovers overlooking the Arno River under the moon. I loved every minute.

We walked back together. In such high heels I needed his arm for support. We separated a block away and entered the hotel separately, then met at the empty bar where he served me wine. I swallowed the first glass in two big gulps.

"I think I'm a little tipsy," I said, after guzzling a second glass of Chianti.

Roberto rolled his eyes or maybe I imagined it. As corny as it sounds, 'Three Coins in the Fountain' music returned in my head.

He's just a waiter, Susan, Mom said as she elbowed herself right smack between us. *Where are your standards? You have a doctor back home.*

Nobody was around so I edged out mom and moved closer to Roberto.

"This has nothing to do with Kevin," I mumbled into Roberto's sleeve.

"What did you say?"

"Nothing," I said, then mumbled, "NOW says my birthday. NOW, or it will be too late."

Roberto had no idea what I meant. Nor did he care. I drank a third glass of wine then walked with determination to the elevator, wobbling in my new red heels, my knees aching while I bit my bottom lip and shook my head trying not to change my mind. My spontaneous haircut worked out well. Maybe this spontaneous something with Roberto would also be fine though I knew it was ridiculous to compare a haircut to what I was about to do. More likely I was inviting horrible consequences that could be devastating to my marriage. I made sure nobody saw us, then followed.

15: Emma Wants Dinner

Momism 15: Be delightful and you will delight others.

Emma wanted to thank Kevin in her own way for such a wonderful new appearance. She called him on his cell phone but he got off so fast she didn't have a chance to say what she wanted to say. It bothered her that he sounded annoyed so she stopped calling. The last thing she wanted to do was irritate this wonderful man. She would figure out another way to get to him.

It was three months since her nose operation and for the past few weeks she had tried to find Dr. Kendall at ballroom dance parties. He had been so cordial and polite when she had introduced him to her mother at the 92nd St. Y. But the parties at the Y were not held often and she was impatient.

She decided to try other dance studios in the city and became part of the New York dance circuit. It was no sacrifice since dancing was her passion. The high-energy swing classes gave her an aerobic workout and the Latin evenings were an opportunity to wear her most sensual outfits.

It wasn't until she went back to the 92nd St. Y that she got lucky. She spotted Dr. Kendall standing in a corner watching the crowd dance, looking at couples circling the enormous room in sync with the music. He appeared to be lost in his own thoughts, there—but not really there.

She followed him with her eyes for a few minutes before approaching. Once again he was cordial and polite but this time he was not as friendly. She never dreamed he might be thinking about his own problems and that his aloof demeanor had nothing to do with her.

She tried to start a conversation but he barely responded and avoided eye contact. Emma didn't see Susan so she asked Kevin to dance. He declined. She continued to stand next to him hoping he wouldn't walk away. Maybe he would feel more comfortable talking to her if he knew she had a boyfriend.

"I miss my boyfriend," she said.

"I understand. I'd be a lot happier if Susan were here," he said. Then he became quiet.

He didn't ask her about her boyfriend so she decided to switch topics.

"I love it," Emma said, as she turned to face him. He appeared perplexed, so she clarified what she meant. "I love my nose. For the first time in my life I love my face. Thank you, thank you, thank you."

He relaxed a bit. "It's always a pleasure when my patients are happy," he said, with half a smile.

Finally, she had gotten him to talk to her. Encouraged, she stepped up her offense. She leaned into him. He stepped back.

"I'd like to thank you in a better way. Dr. Kevin, would you do me the honor of being my guest for dinner?" she asked visualizing her new clingy, backless dress.

Kevin blushed and shook his head no.

"I'm flattered, Emma, but it's not a good idea," he said, trying to be civil. "I don't mean to be rude but I prefer to have dinner with my wife."

She sat down on one of the nearby chairs lining the wall.

"But you've been such a good friend," she said, looking up toward him, knowing it wasn't true.

"I'm not your friend. I'm your doctor," he said. "Get a grip. Or if you need a friend I'll introduce you to my daughter."

It sounded harsh so he tried to soften the message with another half smile.

Emma pouted her best little girl pout then realized how inappropriate it was. She felt as foolish as she looked. What was it about this man that brought out the worst in her? She didn't act this way with other men. She had no interest in befriending any other older people.

Sometimes she felt adrift in the city. Maybe she just wanted a connection with a warm and welcoming local family. If so, Emma figured Susan would be the one to approach, not Dr. Kendall. Besides, neither one of them were particularly welcoming to her. She knew her behavior was counter-productive, but she couldn't stop herself. She was on her own special mission.

"It's just dinner," she said, trying to look more serious. "Maybe you can give me some advice. Maybe you can help me figure out how to get my boyfriend to commit—and how to get my mother to accept my choices. Maybe we can have dinner tomorrow night."

"I'm having dinner with my daughter tomorrow night," he said. "If you want such advice, I think Susan would be a better person for you to talk to. She flew to Europe today and I'll be joining her soon. You can try her when we get back."

He barely looked at her. She kept talking anyway. He never said more than oh, or uh-huh. The music shifted from a cha cha to a waltz and he danced off with someone else he seemed to know.

Emma was frustrated. She had another agenda beyond pure friendship. Maybe if she could get him to go someplace quiet she could ask him something more important. But he hardly spoke to her. This dinner opportunity would be a major challenge.

While he danced around the room Emma saw him looking at her. By the time he returned to her area he thanked his partner and sat down next to her.

"Look, Emma. Maybe I've been too abrupt. I think you understand why it's not right for us to create a friendship," he said. "But there's a lesson here. I learned early if you want something you have to work at it. I'm going to be very honest with you. I work at my marriage and an evening out with a young patient does not fit into the program. You should be working hard at the relationship you have with your boyfriend."

Emma forced herself to concentrate, trying to listen and trying to hear the message the doctor was attempting to convey. She thought she got it but then he started to talk about his life as a child and she became confused.

"Let me tell you a little about myself. When I was a kid, my dad took my older brothers and me to Playland in Rye, New York to drive the bumper cars. No matter how straight I stood, my head did not come up to the horizontal line determining who was allowed in. I had to wait at the gate. I wasn't tall enough for the Dragon Coaster or Ferris wheel either. Aside from miniature golf, my major activity was throwing a ball at some target to win a stuffed animal."

"Okay, I'll wear flats."

"That's not the point," he said, wondering if this girl was a hopeless case of self-involvement.

"I like Susan strutting around in high heels as much as I like her red hair. She's gorgeous. She has a gigantic heart. She's smart, a great mother and my best friend. That's an amazing combination—and we've shared so much over the years. I'm not going to give her one moment of discomfort by going to dinner alone with an attractive young patient."

Emma's mouth tightened into a scowl. She was tired of Susan, first at work and now over one simple little meal.

"I know you hear me," Kevin said while watching her expressions. "But I sense you either aren't listening or you still don't get it."

"I think I understand," Emma said.

Maybe this working hard business was the advice Dr. Kendall was attempting to give her about her boyfriend. Or was working hard his rationale for not accepting her invitation to dinner? She had been smart in school, acing her academic subjects but in life she often was baffled.

"I am listening. I want to hear more," she said.
"I've seen my parents happy in a long marriage but they never speak about how they do it, how they keep each other happy and stay together."

Kevin felt a little silly sitting in a dance hall summing up his early life to Emma. He didn't understand the magnet pulling him toward her. He wasn't sure she grasped the connection between what he was saying and the reason he didn't want to be her friend. The rational side of his brain debated with himself whether or not to continue. Then he kept talking.

"I set up a target in Central Park to practice throwing a ball. I practiced every afternoon between homework and tennis lessons, horseback riding and golf. I practiced tossing a ball with my dad and my brothers. I practiced on Saturday and Sunday."

Remembering his efforts and the success that followed made him smile. He was enjoying his own little story.

"The next time my class went to Playland I won so many stuffed animals everyone on the bus carried one home. The tall kids, the little kids, the mean kids and the nice kids—everyone. I felt great, maybe even like a hero. More important, I understood the real reason I had become so popular for one day. It was because I had worked hard. Get it? Hard work to reach your goals. I vowed to continue to do well and then share my good fortune."

Emma nodded yes to keep him going.

"Maybe that's why I'm able to donate to charities," he said. "I'm not bragging but I'm a donor at The Mount Sinai Hospital annual Crystal Ball, a big donor. I'm glad to help out."

By now Emma thought he sounded pompous. She never heard of the Crystal Ball. She had no idea how many charities competed for donations from the wealthy segment of the city. Was he fishing for a compliment?

"Very impressive but you don't have to impress me. I already like you and I still don't understand why we can't eat a meal together outside of your office."

Kevin was frustrated. There was no middle ground with this girl. There was no way to be friendly without her overstepping boundaries at some point. She was more persistent than Susan, as if that were possible.

"I'm trying to explain I believe all our actions are connected," he said. "Telephone calls can lead to dinner; dinner can lead to other things. My wife is smart. She plans well. Give her a job and she'll create the most efficient way to accomplish it. She's always helping people, making their lives easier. Socially, she's not as secure. She already thinks my friendliness is flirting."

He stood up looking for another familiar face to dance with. Then he changed his mind and sat down again. The music changed to a quick step and he was conflicted. He was one of the better dancers and there was a subtle pecking order at these parties. The more skillful dancers sought each other out and a woman he recognized asked him to dance. She had performed in Latin shows and he wanted to join her. He also wanted to complete his conversation and be done with Emma. He promised the woman the next dance.

"I shouldn't be telling you private details about my wife," Kevin said, turning back to Emma. "All you need to know is that I don't want to upset her."

They paused to watch the dancers switch to an Argentine Tango, another one of Kevin's favorite dances.

"Look, I feel I shouldn't be talking to you outside of my office," Kevin said bluntly.

He didn't mention other thoughts that had been disturbing him all evening, thoughts that had crept into his mind every time he saw Emma. He was fighting an attraction to her. In a similar situation Kevin was confident Susan would do the same.

He loved his wife but when he had said, I do, thirty years ago; he never realized what it would be like to share his bed with the same woman year after year, after year after year. He became quiet again.

Emma stopped pouting. She decided his silence was a good thing. She felt on the verge of getting what she wanted.

"Kevin, everybody needs you—your patients, your wife, your kids, your dog, your charities, your parents who live nearby. You have it all. Nobody needs me. Well, my dog needs me. And the kids I teach to dance need me but I'm replaceable there. I envy you in so many ways."

Kevin was aware that many elderly people often feel left out of the mainstream of life. They need to work at integrating themselves into activities and events near their neighborhoods. He had not thought such alienation could also be a problem for young people, especially those who live in New York but have families far away.

"You have to work at your life," he said, tired of the situation and realizing he was starting to sound repetitive.

"One dinner, Kevin, and I promise I'll stop calling. I'll leave you alone. I promise."

16: Till Divorce Do Us Part

Momism 16: If you play you will pay.

Susan, what have you done? my mother asked. *You better not share this with Kevin. Don't give him some forgive-me-relieve-my-guilt speech. You couldn't keep your legs shut. You better keep your mouth shut. Do you hear me?*

I hear you, mother. I'll keep my mouth shut. This has nothing to do with Kevin. It's totally separate.

I did not want to discuss the evening with anyone, much less my mother even if she was just inside my head. I felt awful, but not for any reason you might imagine.

When Roberto and I walked into my hotel room he flicked on the overhead lights, a spotlight on my imperfections.

"Kevin and I prefer candles," I said, missing the almond fragrance I'd come to associate with our intimate moments.

He ignored my comment. God it was bright. *Okay,* I thought. *I can do this. Okay.* I did a little dance while lifting my black sweater over my head. It got stuck on my chin and covered my head. I tugged it off, tried to fling it across the room but it caught on my diamond wedding ring. Roberto laughed. I crumbled the sweater into a ball then flung it away.

"I've never done anything like this before," I whispered. "I can't believe I'm doing this. I'm really, really doing this."

The moment felt artificial but Roberto was real, stripping faster than he served the morning cappuccino. Part of me watched from a distance. You know how that happens sometimes. Roberto caressed my face. By now we were sitting on the bed, me in my black lace La Perla lingerie, Roberto naked. He threw all the pillows on the floor. I shivered. He touched his chest.

"*Ho un leggero dolore.* I have a slight pain," he said. He touched his stomach, his throat. "Indigestion. I've had this before. The doctor says it's reflux."

"Maybe it's nerves. I'm nervous," I said.

He turned toward me then moved close. I let him pull me down until we were lying side by side. This is my moment, I thought, feeling his breath on my cheek. It smelled. I turned away.

"What's wrong?"

"Nothing—it's just—did you eat garlic?"

"Of course I ate garlic. I'm Italian. *L'aglio* makes you sexy."

That's when my moment changed. His chest was covered in unfamiliar white hair. So much hair! It was heaven to be wanted. Probably how Shirley Valentine felt in a play I saw long ago. But Roberto's body felt wrong. My fantasy was much nicer than anything going on in my upgraded junior suite.

When he tried to kiss me, my eyes stayed open, focusing on the bouquet of red roses on the dresser—reminding me I belonged to Kevin. Did I want to poison my marriage like this?

Suddenly my memories emerged. I was 25 again, working in the Communications Department in the New York office of one of the world's largest advertising agencies.

I was young and tried very hard to master my job. At the same time I admit I enjoyed having a reason to get dressed up. I loved to prance around the halls wearing dark suits, creamy silk blouses, and very high heels. My grandmother's pearls added a touch of class. It was just a few years since I had graduated from college and already I had earned a solid position at the company.

Eager to share my success, I brought my mom to an advertising award show at Lincoln Center. I introduced her to the CEO and reporters from the *New York Times* and *Advertising Age* magazine. My mother was a mixture of pushy and protective. If I sneezed on the phone, she would appear 30 minutes later with penicillin. I shouldn't have been surprised at what happened that night.

The evening began as pure entertainment. Mom wandered about the lobby delighted to watch ponytailed men in tuxedoes and sneakers socializing with women who glitzed by in tight black dresses and lots of bling.

After the screening of the best commercials from around the world I mingled in the lobby with the executives from my company. I could feel my mother's eyes tracking me in the crowd. The corporate business world was not part of her background and I hoped she was proud of me.

As I was leaving to attend a formal dinner, I heard my mom shout from across the lobby, her voice rising above the din of 1,000 people engrossed in a multitude of conversations. "Susan, how can you go out without a coat?"

It was like a stopwatch had shut off all sound and motion. Except her voice. My mother's voice. My mother's sweet voice of concern, the voice I remembered as a child, had morphed into a shrill rattle heard by everyone. Everyone could hear my mother's voice unnerving me in front of my boss, in front of the journalists. This was not the image I had hoped to project.

In the midst of my embarrassment, a good-looking blonde man appeared offering his jacket. I felt an immediate attraction and I started to play with the ends of my hair.

In a newfound burst of energy my mother moved right up to him. "She's gorgeous, isn't she? Her name is Susan. Get her card so you can get your jacket back."

And off she went; content her daughter would be cared for, at least for the evening. It's an aggressive mother story but that's how I met my Kevin.

Cozy in his jacket, I paused to look at my King Arthur with his blue eyes. He was handsome, but short. At 5'8" I had difficulty finding dates tall enough for me to wear heels. This was worse. I figured I was about two inches taller than he was in my bare feet.

"Which agency are you with?" I asked.

"I'm not in advertising," he said. "My roommate is a copywriter at BBDO, the Pepsi agency. I'm his guest. And you?"

I smiled, feeling comfortable with academic or professional conversations. "I'm with one of the Coca-Cola agencies. I handle their public relations. What do you do?"

"I'm a plastic surgeon. I specialize in rhinoplasties. I guess you could say I'm a nose man. My name is Kevin, by the way. Kevin Kendall," he said, handing me his card. "Where are you sitting?"

"Table seven but I'm working tonight. I can't socialize," I said, wondering if his eyes were focusing on the bump in my nose or taking a non-plastic surgeon look at my face.

"Then I'll take your mother's advice and get your card. Keep the jacket until we see each other again. Okay Susan? Susan Gold?" he said, reading my name on my business card.

"Sure," I said, already planning to see him professionally. For years I had wanted to sculpt my nose but my mother had refused to pay for the surgery. She believed I was attractive as I was. She thought my nose added character. For the past three years I had saved ten percent of my salary. Now I could afford to move forward on my vanity issue.

I expected Dr. Kendall to contact me since I had his suit jacket. More important, I had gotten the impression he was interested. By day number eight, when I still hadn't heard from him, I decided to forget any social aspect and made an appointment for a consultation.

"I meant to call you earlier this week," Dr. Kendall said the minute I stepped into his office. "I had three surgeries scheduled and no time to have the nice long conversation I wanted. I decided to wait until I had a free day to take you out to a proper first-date dinner."

I felt better. I handed him his jacket then we shifted to a discussion about my nose. Granted, it wasn't a romantic beginning but it worked for us.

It was slow at first. I fought my feelings when I learned he wasn't Jewish. I had been programmed by my family not to date a man who wasn't of my faith. But I was more into the culture and traditions than any orthodox beliefs.

Kevin's brain, our similar values, our mutual dedication to succeed through hard work—and his skillful hands turned out to be far more important than religion or even height. He called me every night we weren't together until our lives became entwined. I knew he was the person who had my back, as the saying goes. And he was so good to me.

In college I had created a list of foolish priorities I wanted in a husband: someone smart enough to attend an Ivy League school, someone whose grandparents spoke English and someone who knew how to dance. I never thought about how superficial this was.

You were so young, so out of touch with the important elements of a relationship, Mom said. *I thought I had done better teaching you good values. It was a miracle when the two of you evolved into a solid loving couple.*

Marrying Kevin had given me an unexpected bonus—an opportunity to live the "best" in New York. Though I was quite content with a more middle class life, I admit I enjoyed the instant acceptance into Kevin's upper class world. As Mrs. Kendall, I would live on Park Avenue. It meant being able to afford private schools for the kids. And it meant enough money to donate to charities and attend fundraisers in designer clothes. I could easily have done without these perks. I would have married him anyway.

Kevin had attended Buckley, the same private school as Mayor John V. Lindsay and David Rockefeller, Jr. He had learned dance and social etiquette at Miss Adam's sixth grade dance classes at a local church. He stood when a woman entered a room. Later, he graduated from Williams College, then Harvard Medical School. His Scottish family had come to America in the 1800's.

Kevin opened the car door for me and held out my chair in a restaurant—manners that made me feel special.

Kevin thought I was beautiful. He admired my independence and liked my dedication to my career. He didn't care that I was uninterested in cooking. I was grounded with an admirable work ethic. We both knew I could use my public relations contacts and skills to build his reputation.

If his parents were upset that I was not a Christian, they buried their feelings. Nobody said anything, not even while planning the wedding.

On the oversized bed in my upgraded junior suite, my mind flashed rapid scenes from our wedding. I remembered a tartan-clad piper playing the bagpipes as Kevin and his family walked down the aisle. A violin and cello then played Pachelbel's Canon when I walked down with my mom to meet Kevin who waited for me under a makeshift *chuppah*, a symbol of the home we would build together. I'll never forget Kevin's beams of happiness as he watched me float closer to him.

The Pastor was on one side, the reformed Rabbi on the other. After the rings were exchanged a friend read a section from Kahlil Gibran's *The Prophet*.

Kevin stamped his foot on a light bulb wrapped in a large cloth napkin tied with a tartan ribbon. The smashed glass reminded half the guests of the destruction of the Temple in Jerusalem; of the fragility of human relationships and that marriage changes the lives of individuals forever. The other guests knew it was something Jewish.

As far as my mother was concerned, if Kevin broke the glass, it was a Jewish wedding. Kevin's mother welcomed me into their clan by pinning a rosette brooch on my dress.

The tartan-clad piper played as he led the guests back down the aisle. At the tables each woman received a silver horseshoe charm, the customary Scottish wedding commemorative gift of good luck. Then the band broke into a twenty-minute Horah, the traditional Jewish wedding dance.

My mother *kvelled.* There is no English word that comes close to describing the combination of joy and relief she felt. She had married off her daughter to a doctor. Besides, I was already 25. It was time I found a man to take care of me.

And he had taken care of me. We had taken care of each other for 30 years. What was I doing in the Westin Excelsior in Florence wearing skimpy lingerie with a player I would never see again? The damn, 'Three Coins in the Fountain' music that had been resounding in my head switched to the Horah, booming, booming, booming.

Roberto tried to kiss my neck. I uttered a muffled—ugh—and pushed him away. "Out!" I shouted taking action, taking control of the situation and maybe starting to take control of my life.

Roberto got up, naked and limp. He took my hand and kissed it with that same stupid bow. *No more drama,* I thought as he dressed in silence then walked out of the room, closing the door softly behind him.

I stayed in bed, ashamed of my behavior. I hadn't gone through with it. Was it close enough to be considered cheating? When the music in my head stopped I put the roses on the sink near the tub and took a long hot bath. Kevin must never know about tonight.

17: Emma Still Wants Dinner

Momism 17: Let him think he's in control, then do it your way.

Emma stashed her cigarettes in her Gucci look-alike handbag then slipped on her flats rather than her Freed of London dance shoes. Fuck the heels. Dr. Kendall had a thing about being short and she was zooming in on ego gratification, aiming for emotional comfort. When Emma saw him enter Buttenwieser Hall, she ran over to greet him.

"Hello, Emma," he said, and then walked away before she could give him a friendly peck on the cheek. Emma started to follow him, then decided to go to the cash bar in the lounge. She bought two glasses of wine and brought them to where Kevin was standing.

"What's the occasion?" he asked accepting the wine. "Us," she said, trying to clink his glass in a toast.

"I want to entice you to accept my invitation to dinner one evening—an invitation for a night both of us will remember as a turning point in our lives."

He looked at her as if she were out of her mind. There was persistence and there was not knowing when to stop. Just a few months ago he had thought she was adorable and sweet—even sexy. He had worried she would creep into his fantasies at night. Now she was grating on him. He felt relieved. At least the temptation was gone.

"No turning point," he said, over strains of Salsa music. "I'm beginning to think you're crazy."

Emma sat on one of the nearby chairs. "Kevin, you are the calmest man I know. How did you turn out so steady?"

"I told you, I work hard and use my brain as a competitive tool. And I balance it with heart. Heart is very important," he added so he wouldn't sound quite so tough.

"Were you a nerd?" she asked leaning in. He leaned back.

"If staying focused makes you a nerd, then maybe. I always thought of myself as an athlete—in sports without teams. I think I like dancing because it is so athletic. Then there was golf. Early on I joined two country clubs. I encouraged Susan to take up golf."

Kevin placed his wine on the floor. Thinking about what a good sport Susan was about golf made him miss her.

"I'm not going to dinner with you," he said. "I eat dinner with my family. Period. You are hearing but you are choosing not to listen again. I'm here to dance, not meet up with you."

Kevin felt uncomfortable being so direct. It sounded unkind. His upbringing and his nature pushed him to be well mannered. He got up to dance. Emma stood, thinking she would be his partner, but he excused himself then turned to someone else and off they went.

Emma was left mumbling to herself. "I can reserve a table at Nicola's, on East 84th Street," she whispered. "Italian. I figure since I'm asking you out I get to choose the restaurant. We can meet there, if you prefer."

Emma knew this was only a wish and most likely it would never happen. On the other hand, Kevin liked to help people. He had said so. She decided to try once more before giving up. Maybe he could help her work hard with her boyfriend—her boyfriend who should be dancing with her, flying around the room doing lifts and advanced steps. If he were here she wouldn't want advice or anything else from Kevin.

But her boyfriend wasn't there. He was on vacation without her. She waited until Kevin danced closer to her spot then cut in.

"Please, Kevin. If we can't have dinner, can we share a lunch? Just a little time so I can talk to you alone."

"We're talking now. I don't understand why you want a conversation over a meal. What difference would food make?"

"It's not the food. It's a chance to discuss something important without interruptions. You're smart. I know you can help me figure out how to make my relationship better. I want advice about my boyfriend."

"This sounds like a conversation you should be having with Susan, not me," he said.

"I want a man's point of view," Emma said. "Please."

Kevin often had lunch with friends or acquaintances. Susan liked to make her own lunch plans. Kevin sighed. On one side he felt harassed. On the other hand he felt sorry for this young, lost girl. At least lunch came with a cap on the amount of time it took.

"Fine. I'll meet you for lunch at Panera tomorrow from 12:00 to 1:00. Then I need to be back in my office. And after, please don't contact me again. That's it. End of story. Okay?"

18: Dinner Leads to Dancing

Momism 18: Better to dance with your vacuum.

After my bath I wanted to cancel dinner with Giorgio. Since I didn't have his phone number and I'm too respectful to stand someone up, I slipped into my black low-rise pants with the flared leg and a black sweater then dragged myself down to the cocktail lounge. He was waiting for me, also dressed all in black. We looked like we were ready to carry out a heist.

"Are you all set to rock and roll?" he asked snapping his fingers with more enthusiasm than I could tolerate.

"Oh no," I said with a groan, sitting on a bar stool and resting my head on my arms on the bar. "I'm wiped out. I can't do it."

"Visiting Lucca must have been wonderful," he said, not having any idea about my last hour or two. "It's your chance to make a memory—to dance in Florence!" he said, moving his shoulders in a mock dance. When I didn't react he added some hip movements.

"Some wine and pasta will revive you. I organized everything," he said, looking right at me. "Your only job is to enjoy yourself."

He had arranged the evening, just like Kevin would do. Then Giorgio smiled that smile of his. The snarl was gone. I liked the way his wavy hair met the top of his collar and his friendly eyes flashed with an air of mischief. He looked adorable again.

I gave in. Must be part of my DNA. Even in Florence with someone I hardly knew, I was giving in. Same old me. The only difference in this scenario was the foreign environment and my out-of-character perky short haircut.

Less than an hour later we were getting out of a taxi at the YAB Disco close to the Piazza della Repubblica. Rows of motorcycles were parked on the nearby streets. There was a long line of kids with tattoos milling beneath a sign. Judging from the boys' baby faces under shaved heads or spiked hair they were in their twenties, though the majority didn't seem old enough to drive. The girls looked even younger in extreme minis, high heels or boots. Some wore sneakers. Most had either very short haircuts or below shoulder-length hair.

Eventually we entered a smoke-filled room, crowded with more young people. Miley Cyrus blared 'Let's Dance' on the loud speaker. Then the music shifted to hard rock. Girls with pink or green streaks in their hair smiled at Giorgio as he pushed into the crowd. I noticed he smiled back, seemingly at home in the noisy environment.

The pain in my bunion flashed like a yellow traffic light warning me of what might come next. My pants seemed dated, my new hairdo tame. Even Giorgio looked mature compared to the other dancers moving under purple lights. I rubbed my foot as he tried to pull me onto the dance floor.

The kids' dance movements were jerky. Arms flailed in the air. Nobody made eye contact. People stuck out their butts and lifted their knees. Men held their crotches. This was not dancing, or at least not what I had learned in ballroom classes. There was no framed posture, no body contact. I stood still.

"Wait here. I'll be right back," Giorgio said.

"No. Don't leave me with these kids. Please, please don't go."

It was too late. He was gone and I felt lost. Then the music shifted to a waltz. The crowd grumbled, stopped the jerky movements, and complained in Italian.

By then Giorgio was back at my side. He lifted his arms in a formal dance position. The crowd faded from my vision. I was in my own bubble with beautiful music and a handsome partner. I accepted his invitation with a gentle nod. I placed my hand in his. He put his hand high up on my back and we started to glide, hesitantly at first, then full of grace. I was Ginger Rogers. He was my Fred Astaire. We must have looked like pros, or entertainers, because the kids quieted down, then backed off giving us space. They didn't know what to do with this music so they watched. Maybe they liked what they saw.

The waltz morphed into a Paso Doble. The crowd formed a circle around us. My exhaustion lifted. Not everyone can do this lively, sexy dance that is modeled after a Spanish or Portuguese bullfight. Kevin is a good dancer but Giorgio was better. The crowd cheered as we moved at rapid speed around the room. I wished I had on a flowing skirt and my open-toe dance shoes with the strap across the top.

The music shifted again, this time to a tango, my favorite. We danced with attitude, slow, slow, slow, quick, quick. My head was buried in Giorgio's shoulder, our legs entangled in perfect rhythm. I felt young.

His posture was amazing, his arms strong. It was as if we had rehearsed for hours. Even without the proper shoes I knew we looked professional. I wasn't surprised when the crowd applauded. Giorgio helped me bow and gave me a hug. My arms lingered around his waist.

I could feel my mom next to us. *Calm down, Susan. Remember, you're married,* she said, while I imagined she removed my hands from Giorgio's waist. *In New York and in Italy married. Kids married. Even if you were in Vegas married. Enjoy the dance, and then it's no thanks and go home married.*

I was too joyful to pay any attention to her. "Giorgio, you are astounding! Where did you learn to dance like that?"

"I'm full of surprises, no?"

"For sure. And so delightful. I wish we could keep dancing. And touring around Florence. Too bad I'm going to Venice."

"You're leaving me?" he said in mock horror while he placed his hands on his heart. "So soon?"

"Day after tomorrow. I plan to visit the Biennale Art Show—to see the Sophie Calle exhibit."

"Who?"

"Sophie Calle. She's a French contemporary artist," I said, well my tone was condescending.

"Will your husband meet you there?"

"That's the plan."

"So—we have tomorrow night. That's good because I want to show you a special place."

"Where?" I asked.

"Artimino. It's an Etruscan village high in the hills. Spectacular."

Susan, it's good to see you smile, my mother said. *Now bring your smile to Venice—or bring Kevin to Artimino.*

19: Psychobabble Is Free

Momism 19: Don't believe everything you hear.

I was humming as we walked into the hotel around 2:00 AM. Giorgio scooted right up to his room. I stopped when I glanced to the right and saw Roberto sitting at the bar waving for me to join him. Would this night never end?

Instead of his waiter's jacket, he was wearing a gray long-sleeved shirt with the top button open allowing bits of his curly white hair to peak out. I knew he was on the breakfast shift so something was not right. I walked to the bar to find out what he wanted.

"*Susanna*, I must speak to you," he said, jumping up. "I must say good-bye in a better way. Let me buy you a drink."

I guess he was embarrassed about the time in my room but I didn't care. I was on a dancing high and had no interest in being brought down by a conversation with anyone, especially a married player.

"Please, it's very late. I'm exhausted," I said. "I'm sorry about earlier—I've never done anything like that before. Thought about it but never did it."

My thoughts tumbled out on automatic pilot. Words connected to words like train cars on a high-speed trip.

"By myself in a new environment I thought I could but I can't. It's too far out of my comfort zone. It's way too far removed from my traditional life. Most important, I really love my husband."

I felt so stupid, especially since I had just been out dancing with Giorgio.

"Of course you do," Roberto said as if he comprehended what I was saying. In addition to the language barrier, I was babbling. I was sure Roberto didn't understand as much as he pretended.

"I'd rather be alone right now," I said. I could see the distress on his face and softened. *Why leave him with a bruised ego? I hope he doesn't think we're going to try again.* I thought.

"Thank you for wanting me," I said. "You have no idea how much it meant. In a strange way it ended my quest for—how shall I say this—for another experience."

Mom appeared on a bar stool holding a scotch on the rocks. *He should be thanking you. Where did I go wrong?*

I ignored her and felt awake again. I did not want to go up to my room yet.

"I changed my mind," I said. "I'll have a drink but let's stay here. I am meant to be faithful to the man I love. I can't break any more moral rules. I don't want to hurt Kevin."

"But Kevin's not here. He won't know and besides, this isn't about Kevin. This is about you," Roberto said, in his thick Italian accent. "You must learn to take care of yourself."

Yuck, I thought. I can't bear more meaningless psychobabble. I pushed the conversation into something a bit more solid.

"Roberto, I bet I'm not the first tourist you approached. Don't you worry that your time with other women will lead to a divorce?"

Roberto smiled, cavalier. He didn't seem to mind my personal question.

"Divorce is not an option. I made a commitment under God. Besides, being with you is not cheating on my wife. My life is with her. I am happy at home."

"I don't get it. How can you believe what we almost did was not cheating?"

Roberto moved closer. "*Il mio cuore e' puro.* My heart is pure. That's what counts."

His philosophy seemed like an excuse to cheat without feeling guilty. I felt guilty just standing near him. My eyes teared. Roberto gave me another clean handkerchief. I wondered how many he carried.

Sure, I thought with sarcasm then gave lip service to his sermon. Whatever he said was irrelevant and a bit silly.

"I'll tell you a secret," he said. "My wife and I sing in the shower. Try it. Concentrate on the melody, the lyrics. You'll forget all your problems. If you sing together in the shower, you will have *un grande amore.*"

"Okay, okay, I'll sing in the shower—with Kevin. But I still don't get it."

He shrugged his shoulders without a comment.
It had been a long evening of too many out-of-marriage happenings. I was tired and emotional.

"You don't know your strength, your attraction," he said. "I think you are too special to have such pain."

"Something is missing," I said, thinking about my job and how it had filled my days. "I don't know how to fix it."

I recognized how odd and mixed up I must have sounded. I guess it made no difference. For my own sake, I kept explaining, hoping I would understand myself.

"When a man retires everyone worries about him," I said. "When a woman retires, nobody reacts. I'm too old to start over. I don't know where I belong. I thrive on hard work. Now I have no work."

Roberto looked confused. "Retire? What does that have to do with love?"

I knew Roberto didn't understand but it was okay. I was figuring it out for myself while talking at him. Then he surprised me with his attempt at insight. He had been listening. Genuinely listening.

"You belong inside your skin," he said, serving up more psychobabble.

I stared at him and almost laughed. He looked at his watch, a not-too-subtle glance he thought I wouldn't notice.

"*Susanna,* I told my wife I left my watch at the hotel. I must go home."

"It's a bit late to retrieve your watch when you are coming here tomorrow morning for work. Did she believe your explanation?"

"We have a good marriage. She never questions anything I tell her."

He tried to hug me but I jerked back. There was no electricity between us and I was glad when he pulled away.

"I enjoy you," he said, as if I had not just rejected him. "You have an aura about you, a special radiance."

He took my hand and led me to the back lobby. Mom followed.

"Look at this ceiling." He pointed above, appearing more confident. "The light shines behind the stained glass. It brings out the colors, its grandeur. You must do the same. You must turn on your light."

I could hear Mom say, *Give me a break here. How corny can one get? And how often has he said this to other women at the hotel?*

In New York I would have mocked such a conversation, assuming I would even allow it to happen. This evening, I decided to just go with it, as they say.

Roberto took both my hands in his. Mom snorted.

"Life is an attitude. If you don't like something you cannot change, change your attitude," Roberto said. "You're the boss. You're in control."

Wait a minute, Mom said. *That's what I always tell you.*

"It sounds too simple," I said.

"It is that simple."

I stared at the ceiling. Roberto stood behind me. He put his arms around me, nuzzled my cheek, my neck. It might sound sexy but my mind was already out of this adventure. My skin crawled and I felt he was overstepping a boundary.

I pulled away gently enough not to hurt his ego yet strong enough to make a clean break. I put my hands in my pants pocket in case he tried to kiss my hand. Instead, he bowed dramatically with a nod and eye contact. Mom bowed too. I shook my head.

I was done. End of story.

20: Dazzled By Artimino

Momism 20: Jewish girls don't ride motorcycles.

The next day I met Giorgio as planned. Outside the hotel a black two-seater Vespa motor scooter glistened in the late afternoon sun. Compared to the other motorcycles parked nearby it seemed like a toy. Giorgio held two helmets and I knew he expected me to ride behind him.

"I can't do this," I said. "I get no kick out of danger. If you want us to go somewhere, lets take a cab. A cab is much safer."

By now his helmet was secured on his head with a few strands of his dark hair slipping seductively onto his forehead. I was aware of how cute he looked. He held out the other helmet to me. I backed away.

"Come, on," he coaxed, cheery as always. "We are going to a medieval hamlet called Artimino. It is just outside of Florence."

His mild foreign accent, mischievous eyes and upbeat demeanor pulled me in—again.

"There is La Ferdinanda, the Medici Villa known as the villa of the hundred chimneys because it has many chimneys, one in every room. I believe the Villa is now a UNESCO World Heritage site. Many couples have their weddings there.

He sounded like a tour guide but I was interested. And I admit, I was happy to see a place that wasn't on Kevin's list, a place I could introduce to him.

"The area is steeped in history," Giorgio said. "We'll take a glorious ride, Italian style and make a memory."

I knew Giorgio thought that would entice me but all it did was make me wish Kevin was with us and the memory I was going to make would be with my husband.

Over the years Kevin had asked me to step over my shadow and bury my fears. He had wanted me to try new experiences with him. Many times I had refused. I was afraid and stubborn.

If I agreed to a ride on the Vespa with Giorgio I felt like I would be cheating my husband out of a new experience that belonged to him. Once again, I felt guilty. How could I do something so out of character with someone else?

Giorgio insisted. We argued back and forth until I gave in. I had wanted four days on my own to have an adventure and I convinced myself this was part of it. Still scared, I mounted the back of the bike with little confidence and far less grace.

"Hold on," he said.

I didn't move.

"Hold on or you might fall off," he said.

I put my arms around him.

"Tighter."

I strengthened my grip aware that my uplifted breasts were digging into his back. He turned with his signature crooked smile. "Not bad," he said.

"Okay. I'm okay. Really, I'm okay," was all I could whisper more to myself than to him. Then off we went, pulling onto the main road along the Arno River, while I hummed 'Rock Around the Clock' in my head over the noise of the traffic. "How far is it?" I yelled.

"About half an hour, depending upon traffic. First we go west toward Pistoia then, at Poggio a Caiano, we will turn south and climb up to Artimino."

"I can barely hear you." I took deep breaths, in and out, concentrating as if I were meditating. I tried to alleviate my anxiety with a song but the wind filled my mouth until I coughed. When he tilted to the left as the road curved, I panicked and clutched his waist as hard as I could hoping not to fall off. I was even more frightened when he turned his head toward me instead of looking at the road.

Giorgio shouted to be heard. "There are olive trees and vineyards and Carmignano wine," he said, sounding like a tour guide again, spouting out what he had grown up with—or maybe memorized to impress me. "The farm has over 121 hectares or close to 300 acres and a small hotel and apartments for rent."

A car behind us honked so we moved to the right, hugging the side of the hill as far away as we could from the edge of what seemed like a cliff. Another car came toward us down the narrow road. Once again we edged closer to the side of the hill. I was beyond afraid.

"Hang on. We are almost at the ristorante in the area," Giorgio said, as if the end of this ten-mile drive from Florence was normal and ordinary. He then picked up speed and passed the car that had just passed us. Not my style of driving, for sure.

The wind mixed with the sound of the motor. I put my head—my helmet on his back. I could picture Mom passing us in a taxi, shouting from the passenger seat, *Susan, get off. Jewish girls don't ride motorcycles.*

I squeezed Giorgio. My eyes were as wide open as possible. The narrow road became narrower. Turns were steep, sharp. The car in front pulled over to make room for another car approaching from the opposite direction. It was also hugging the side of the cliff to avoid the edge of the road. I hoped it wouldn't plow into us. The two-way street felt wide enough to be a one-way street but somehow all the vehicles managed to avoid a catastrophe. I trembled knowing we had to drive back down after dinner.

By the time we reached a high wall made of stone at the top of the area, I was exhausted though I hadn't done a thing. I needed to lean on Giorgio to maintain my balance when I dismounted. A wild boar with a huge body and stubby legs snorted while tearing at a grape vine behind a fence.

"That's one ugly animal," I said staring at its dark brown hairy face. While it used its large tusks to excavate roots and forage for insects, I saw hoof prints made by other boar.

"They taste good," Giorgio said laughing. "And I don't think it's just one."

He was right. There were at least ten more wiggling, munching on the low greenery. I felt itchy looking at them.

"Ugh!" I said, then walked up a cobblestone hill linking Giorgio's arm with affection and familiarity. The path was lined with giant clay pots filled with vibrant pink flowers, a peaceful antidote to the ride up. We walked through an iron gate attached to a stone arch. From there we could view a medieval town.

Giorgio had promised spectacular but this was far more dazzling than anything I had imagined. I've never seen such late afternoon sun bouncing off green and silver leaves of olive trees or so many shades of green fields bordered by cypress trees or forests and rows of grape vines. Towns dotted the valley below with red-roofed buildings clustered around churches. Nearby was the villa with its glorious chimneys.

I became obsessed to share my experience. First I took iphoto shots of the villa with its stucco walls that were peeling ever so slightly. I captured some of the chimneys and the dramatic graceful staircase sweeping down to the fertile lawn. And I took photos of the statues of lions. I sent them all to Jenny. Then I punched in email messages on my phone.

"Are you e-mailing Kevin?" Giorgio asked.

"Yes, about Artimino—but not about you. I haven't told him about you—yet. And I'm emailing Jenny. She's looking up all the places I visit. It's like she's here with me."

"Susan, you are so close to your family. I'm jealous," he said, as we walked toward the terrace of Ristorante Da Delfina. We ordered a Spritz, a combination of Prosecco, Aperol, sparkling mineral water and a slice of orange. We sat there enjoying our orange-colored icy drinks while marveling at the green hills rolling below until the restaurant opened at 7:30.

Giorgio was jealous. This surprised me. I assumed he saw his family on a monthly or even weekly basis. You know the stereotype: Italian, family, food.

"Don't you see your family every week, Italian style?" I asked.

"No. It's impossible. They are far away."

"Where? Where are they now?"

He flicked his wrist to dismiss the question and I let it pass, reminding myself I'd never see him again. Though I was curious, it wasn't important to me and he had a right to his privacy.

It got dark. The lights twinkled in the houses in the towns below. It was magical. I didn't want to get up when the maître'd came to escort us to our reserved table inside.

We walked through one of the dining rooms passing by an enormous open wood-burning fireplace with the fragrance of dinner options filling the room. Heavy tables covered in white cloths were decorated with pink flowers in tiny glass vases. In the center of each table were containers of olive oil and vinegar, salt and pepper and toothpicks. Colorful ceramic plates hung on the walls. It smelled so good I immediately erased the anxiety I had suffered on the ride up.

A waiter held out one of the dark, wooden, straight-backed chairs with wicker seats. Once settled, Giorgio ordered some deep red Camignano wine. *I'm glad he's taking the lead,* I thought. I stretched my legs out under the table. Finally, I was beginning to relax.

Giorgio ignored the menu again and ordered in English sprinkled with a little Italian. It was much easier to understand him than Roberto.

"We will have the house specialty *pappardelle al ragu cinghiale* then *carciofi* and beef Florentine with *fagioli cannellini,*" he said.

He turned to me to translate. "Pasta first, then artichokes and steak Florentine with cannellini—white kidney beans." It was the first time I heard him speak so much Italian though most of the Italian words he used were to describe the sumptuous dishes we were to eat. The pasta was better than at Elio's, over on Second Avenue, or the spaghetti dishes Kevin and I make at home.

"Mmm. Do you have any idea what's in this?" I asked, gorging on mouthful after mouthful instead of picking at my food as I often do. *The hell with Weight Watchers,* I thought.

"Pasta with carrots, onions, celery, tomato, wine, garlic and," he said, then paused for effect, "wild boar."

I controlled my impulse to spit out the heaping mouthful. In truth, it was delicious and once again, I thought of all the times Kevin had asked me to taste something unusual and I had refused.

When I had walked through the arched passageway I felt like I had walked back in time at Artimino. Now I wished I could go back in time with Kevin and be more open to his suggestions.

After dinner, I held onto Giorgio's arm for balance as we strolled back down the cobblestone hill. By now it was even darker and the moon offered the best light. It was so lovely as we ambled beyond the parking area toward an olive grove. An aging buxom woman in a scarf and black dress rushed from her house. She resembled the peasants in some Italian films. She screamed at us, *"Vai. Vai. Scio."*

"She reminds me of my Russian-born grandmother," I said. "When I was a little girl, my younger sister and I summered with our grandparents in Bethlehem, New Hampshire."

"Where's that?"

"In the White Mountains—the northeast part of the country. I was embarrassed because they spoke Russian and Yiddish. I wanted to be all-American and not be saddled with a different language and a different culture."

By now we had turned away from the woman's olive grove and were close to the motor scooter. It's funny how something small and unexpected can trigger a flood of memories that has little to do with the present moment. That's what the peasant woman did for me. We were well beyond her but the visions exploded in my head and begged to be told.

"By the time I was eight, I was the one who asked for tomatoes or milk in the general store," I said. "I learned to be in charge. Loved the grown-up feeling."

"It seems like you did very well," Giorgio said, sounding more polite than interested.

That didn't stop me from rambling on. The two of us were no longer unfamiliar but we still had very little in common. Sharing these memories was as good as any other conversation we might have.

"I don't know how well I did," I said, following up on his comment. "I wasn't allowed to hike the trails because I could be trampled by a moose—or attacked by bears. Then there were home remedies from the old country. If I sprained my ankle, I had to soak it in vinegar. If I coughed, my grandparents put Gulden's mustard on my chest."

I had not thought about my grandparents in such a long time. I felt connected to my roots by pulling up these details.

"I never embraced their differences, never valued their culture," I said, still reminiscing.

Giorgio was quiet. Perhaps he was listening. Perhaps not. It didn't matter. I continued to talk as he put on his helmet.

"You're quite the chatterbox today," he said, while I stood like an obedient child allowing him to adjust the strap to my helmet.

"I know. I just can't stop thinking about my past," I said. "At one point early in our courtship, when I was young and foolish, I believed Kevin could rescue me from my background, from being the grandchild of immigrants. Now I like my personal history. I feel proud of the challenges my ancestors overcame, leaving Russia to start over in America. It's not a new or unique story, but it's mine."

"I can relate to that," Giorgio said. "If I settle in America to be with my girlfriend, I shall have to adopt a different culture like your grandparents did. I worry about it. I wonder how hard it would be to become an immigrant."

I was relieved to get a comment from him. Any comment, rather than the silence my musings seemed to inspire. I wondered if I would see him again if he moved to America.

"I think life has been easier for Kevin," I said. "His great grandparents were born in New York. As I mentioned, he's a doctor. He'll never force mustard remedies on us, though he's also protective like my grandparents were."

"Because he loves you, no?"

"Absolutely," I said. "My mother was protective, too. Over protective."

That's right, said my mom. *Blame your mother. Why is it always the mother?* I waved her away.

Giorgio nodded his head choosing silence again. Only he knew if he understood me or was lost in his own thoughts. I played with the few wisps of my hair that stuck out of my helmet, twisting the ends into curls. And I kept talking.

"At home, Kevin's in charge."

"I don't believe it," Giorgio said. "You said you were in charge at work. Why not at home? At least part of the time?"

I shrugged. "I don't know why. It's just the way it evolved," I said. "I guess I gave him power at home. At work I thought my title gave me strength. I was the *Director* of Public Relations. It made me feel strong. Now that's gone."

"So do something else. I'm sure your husband isn't in love with you because of your job. Nobody likes you because of your title. That's such a ridiculous idea."

Why was everyone smarter than me when it came to my life? Why could Giorgio and Roberto disperse advice while I was a mystery to myself? Maybe it was time to ask myself some better questions.

Giorgio looked at his watch. "It's late. We should head back." He mounted the Vespa.

"From what you've told me over these few days you have it all—husband, kids, travel—even a dog. I bet you have a nice apartment, too. It looks like you have a blessed life yet you complain more than the poor woman in the book you carry, *History: A Novel*. Ida had good reason to complain. Her life was sparse and often in danger."

I felt foolish. He was right, of course, but emotions and feelings don't always follow what is rational.

"You live in America, the land of diversity, acceptance of many religions, or acceptance of none. You're beautiful and healthy. You lost your job but you can afford to keep your lifestyle and do something else. You can even do nothing. What a luxury! Why complain?"

"Ouch!" I said, startled at the blunt way he summed up my good fortune. "I thought I was just stating facts. I didn't mean for them to come out as complaints."

"Forgive me, but I think you're spoiled," he said. "You're running from what you call the illusion of perfection while searching for an identity you already have. You need some perspective."

"Even if you are right, my pain is real," I said, getting defensive. "For the past three months, I've been like a ghost. Only my retired friends understand. In my gut, I know everyone else thinks like you so I keep quiet, living in a fog. Even Kevin doesn't understand."

There was my mother also dispersing advice. *Susan, you have everything I've ever wanted for you,* she said. *Be happy.*

I swung my leg over the motor scooter. It was easier this time. Though it was dark, we would be able to see the headlights of other cars approaching before they came close to us. It would be safer and more relaxing going back.

"You have been in Italy just three days," Giorgio said. "Dancing and dining last night and riding a motor scooter this evening. So you see, you can be spontaneous. I bet you feel a little better than you did a few days ago, yes? And you still have one more day and night to explore Florence."

"I do feel a little better, thanks to you. Though I don't understand how it happened. And what about you? You have a girlfriend in New York. If you love her so much, what are you doing here with me? I know I asked you before, but why isn't she here?"

Giorgio turned somber. I waved my wrist in the air like he did the other times I hit delicate topics. By now I was very curious. There was something mysterious and exotic about this man. I had grown fond of him and I wanted to know all the details.

"Let me guess," I said. "It's a long story. But before I leave Florence, I'm going to hear it all."

21: Emma Wants Information

Momism 21: Never force anything.

"I love the coffee here," Kevin said, when he met Emma at Panera. With all his resolve not to see this woman, he couldn't believe he had caved in and agreed to a lunch. Maybe it was because underneath all the bravado, he felt Emma was a nice girl who was a little forlorn in New York. Perhaps he could help her. On the other hand, he was glad it would be just for one hour.

"I like this place. It's close to my apartment. And the food is good," she said, touching his arm.

Kevin felt a jolt of electricity and became alarmed. He thought the attraction had disappeared but now he wasn't sure. He noticed Emma's dress was too short and too tight.

Susan knew how to be sexy and elegant. Emma was sexy in a trying-too-hard way, an impossible-to-pretend-any-innocence style. All of a sudden being together made him nervous. What would he say if one of Susan's friends appeared? He chose a seat at a table facing the door so he could observe the other patrons as they came inside.

Emma sipped her coffee, put down the half-filled large cup and placed her hands around it.

"Kevin, I think you are one of the smartest men I've ever met."

He felt himself blush then nodded yes, meaning he heard her. He wondered what she would come up with next.

"Kevin, I love your hair and blue eyes. You have such beautiful features. I like your voice."

"This sounds a bit creepy, Emma. What are you up to?" he asked. The hour was going to be worse than he had anticipated.

"Well, from your photos in your office and our brief conversations, I know you play golf and you must enjoy music since you like to dance. But I want to know so much more. What else do you like? What books do you read?"

Kevin was flustered. This was nonsense and none of her business. If he carved out time from his hectic schedule for lunch, it should be for lunch with his daughter. He had little free time and many patients to think about. He was sorry he had agreed to meet Emma. What was he thinking?

"Read?" He put his finger inside his shirt collar and pulled it. "Susan's the reader in the family. She goes through a book a week, mostly fiction."

Emma smiled, sipped more coffee and waited for him to continue.

"Why do you want to know what I read? Is this some sort of test?" he asked. "You don't want to know if I'm a Democrat or Republican or worse, what my astrological sign is, do you?"

"No, of course not. You have no idea what I'm thinking, you know, I mean or where this is headed."

"Headed? I thought this was an opportunity for us to figure out how to get your boyfriend to commit. You're dishing out mixed messages."

Emma pouted. "What do you mean?" she asked, though she knew exactly what he meant.

"First, you're wearing a seductive outfit."

"Thank you for noticing."

"It wasn't a compliment," he said, softening his comment with half a smile.

She looked down, pretending to be hurt.

"Second, we could easily have had this conversation at the 92nd Street Y. It was not necessary for us to meet here."

"I know, it's noisy. That's why I had hoped for a quiet dinner," she said.

"Emma, you can't be as dense as you come off. Sometimes we talk and I feel like I'm listening to a young woman who has some problems with work or relationships and is a little lonesome in New York. I see you as someone trying her best to get back to her better values. I felt that when I saw you with your mother. I admired how you tried to make her feel at ease in a strange environment. I'm fond of that person." Kevin said, biting into his oversized BLT sandwich piled high with roasted turkey and avocado on whole grain bread.

"Other times, like right now, I feel as if I am with someone playing the role of a vixen, someone who will trample people, manipulate anyone, do anything to get what she wants. Which is it? Which one are you?"

"I'm a friend interested in you as a father."

This was a surprise to Kevin. He had thought she was trying to come on to him in a very sexy, obvious and immature way. Suddenly, he felt old.

"You think of me as a father to you?"

"No. I mean you like being a dad, don't you?" She finished her coffee and went to get a refill.

"Dad?" he said, when she returned. "Well yeah. I'm involved—coached soccer, taught the kids to ride bikes, play golf, helped with college essays. You saw the photos in my office. I'm damn proud of my kids, too. Sean is in medical school. Jen has a great job and is in a serious relationship with a guy we like. But why do you ask?"

22: Helmets Save Lives

Momism 22: Things happen for a reason.

We motored at a leisurely pace down the hill from Artimino, hugging the edge of the cliff. It was dark so when a wild boar scooted out from the woods we didn't see it until we were very close. Giorgio swerved, losing his balance. He almost toppled us. The frightened hairy pig snorted and raced around, circling closer, squealing louder than the motor scooter.

"Watch out! Stop!" I yelled, but it was too late. The Vespa crashed head on into the startled animal. I was flung up, up, up off the bike and into the air. By chance I landed in a small patch of soft grass on the side of the road opposite the perilous cliff.

I could hear Giorgio moan. I lay quietly for many minutes assessing what had happened. My helmet was still on. My blouse was torn but there was no blood oozing out, no pain. I wiggled my toes. They were fine. I moved my fingers. All were okay. I blinked my eyes, turned my head to the left, then right. I was stunned but I wasn't hurt.

My mom extended her hand to me. *Jewish girls and motorcycles...I told you,* she said.

"Oh, shut up already," I said. I had never said shut up to my mother. Maybe it was a sign I was ready to break from her, finally in middle age, ready to make my own decisions and be happy with them. Of course, Mom needed the last word in this discussion.

Don't say shut up to your mother. After all I've done for you!

I rolled over and got up, shaken. Really shaken. I've never been in an accident before. I could have been killed. I needed Kevin.

I heard Giorgio moan again. He was on his back in the middle of the road next to the wounded boar. Blood covered Giorgio's face and hands. He moaned again and again.

"Don't move," I said, shifting into mother mode. I held his hand, rubbed his fingers, smoothed the hair on his forehead much like I would do for my son, Sean.

"We'll get help," I said, though I wasn't sure how. I didn't know an emergency number to call for an ambulance in Italy and Giorgio wasn't speaking. His eyes were wide open and he looked frightened.

I missed Kevin. I missed folding into his shoulders. I wanted him to take over.

By now cars blocked the narrow road in both directions. Drivers honked, yelled, waved their arms out the window. A few got out and rushed to Giorgio. It was a scene.

One man spoke to me in Italian then switched to broken English. He warned me about other angry boars, said they could be dangerous. I didn't see any others but I wasn't sure what I would do if I did. I didn't dwell on the possibilities because I was more concerned about trying to help Giorgio.

Within minutes I heard a siren. Someone must have called 118, the emergency number in Italy. An ambulance was on its way and boy, was I grateful!

The white and orange ambulance, with *Misericordia di Prato* written in blue across the side, was able to bypass the stalled traffic by inching into the edge of the woods. Workers in turquoise and lime yellow jackets lifted Giorgio onto a stretcher and carried him to the ambulance. I walked alongside, one hand holding Giorgio's hand the other clutching my handbag. Giorgio's eyes were closed but he was breathing. Inside the ambulance a doctor, or intern, was took his blood pressure.

The Vespa was in good shape. I knew I would have to organize its return and hoped the police would help me.

In a minute the siren was back on and we were racing down the curved road into Prato, a nearby town with a large, modern, new public hospital.

23: Men Stink

Momism 23: You sound like Doris Day.

"Signora, are you this man's mother?" asked Simona, the nurse in the *Ospedale della Misericordia e Dolce* in Prato a few kilometers from Artimino.

"Mother! No. No, I'm not his mother." The question made me realize how much of a visible age difference there was between Giorgio and me.

Do you want to call his family?" she asked. At least I think it's what she asked. It wasn't clear because she spoke to me in a combination of broken English and rapid Italian.

It took some time before I found my English/Italian dictionary buried behind my wallet, my make-up, my phone, my passport, a hairbrush, sunglasses, reading glasses, tissues, crossword puzzles, pens, Purell and my beloved Kindle.

I had an Italian/English app on my phone but it was faster for me to look in the dictionary than to figure out yet another technical application. At the ad agency, tech issues were always assigned to my young staff. Of course, I no longer had a staff. I knew there was much to learn. I just hadn't done it yet.

While I leafed through my little dictionary the nurse looked impatient, but what could I do? I leaned against the antiseptic white wall and skimmed through my book. It was so small it was impossible to read. Once again I rummaged through my handbag until I found what I needed.

"I'm his aunt," I said. I figured it would be better if I claimed to be a relative. I tried to figure out a whole sentence from my dictionary.

"*Sono Americana. Lui e' Italiano ma sono sua zia*—his aunt."

The nurse ignored what I said. Maybe I didn't say it correctly.

"In Italy we believe the right to health is a fundamental human right," she said in broken English. "Our National Health Service covers our citizens."

She stopped talking and looked at me with what I interpreted to be sympathy, but who knows what actually was behind her expression. And why was she spouting information about Italy's National Health Service?

"His driver's license, in his wallet," she said, "his passport in his pocket— *Signora*—he is not Italian. We will help him anyway, but he must pay the ticket, the co-pay fee. It is not much but he must pay."

"What do you mean he's not Italian? He's a professor at the University of Bologna," I said, wishing I could lay down in Kevin's arms and go to sleep. I wanted to rest my head on Kevin's shoulder and make this nightmare go away.

"Giorgio teaches Italian literature," I said. "We talked about books."

"*Signora*, my English is not good," Simona said. "Do you want to pay for him?"

I took out my credit card and hoped to pay the monthly bill before Kevin had a chance to see it. Damn, how did I get myself into a situation involving so many secrets? Keeping information from my husband felt much worse than my befriending a young man. If I had told Kevin about Giorgio on day one, I wouldn't feel as if I had to hide him now.

"How bad is his injury?" I asked the nurse. It was a relief to see she appeared to understand my question.

"Well, *signora, lui e' fortunato. Un mucchio di sangue.* A lot of blood. He will live but with a big scar." She drew an imaginary line from her eye to her mouth. "We will help but he must stay overnight."

"Do you have a plastic surgeon on staff?" I asked, thinking about Kevin again and trying to block out the fact I could have been killed or crippled.

"I am sorry *signora, parla Italiano?*"

She already knew I didn't speak Italian. Why was she asking me?

"No," I screamed. My voice echoed in the vacant corridor. Where was everybody? Why was the place so empty? Were private hospitals more crowded than public ones? This didn't feel anything like an emergency room in Manhattan.

"You have a friend? Someone who speaks Italian and English?" she asked.

"No. I am alone," I said, grasping that it no longer seemed romantic or exciting to be alone.

Kevin always had my back. I always knew we were lucky to have each other but right now I felt it deep in my gut. I flipped through my dictionary but had trouble focusing even with my glasses.

"Sono sola."

"Signora, your nephew, is that how you say it, *lui ha bisogna di una bella dormita adesso.* He must sleep. It is late. Come back early tomorrow morning. We will discharge him early."

The only other person I knew in Italy was Roberto. At least he spoke English but I didn't have his phone number. I didn't even know his last name. Still, I had to reach him. Maybe he would come to the hospital and translate for me. It sounded like all Giorgio needed was sleep but maybe more decisions would have to be made. Maybe I should call Giogio's girlfriend in New York, if he let me.

I touched my torn blouse. I could take a taxi to Florence, change clothes and see if the hotel would contact Roberto for me. I bet he could arrange his schedule to be at the hospital before his breakfast shift. So much for never seeing him again.

The hotel was less than thirty minutes away. The nurse called a taxi for me. I arrived at the Excelsior just as Roberto was leaving work. He had taken an evening shift. I was so relieved I spilled out my story at double speed.

"Slow down, *Susanna. Tu sei confusa.* You are confused."

I tried to slow down but it was impossible.

"We rode a Vespa to Artimino. I know, you warned me not to go. So did my mother."

"*Sua madre.* Is she here too?"

I waved away the question. "Never mind. We hit a wild pig. Giorgio was hurt. Blood everywhere."

"*Stai bene?* Are you okay?"

"Yes, yes. But Giorgio is in the hospital. The Central Emergency Group sent him to the *Ospedale della Misericordia e Dolce a Prato* and I don't understand the nurse. Will you come with me to translate? I wouldn't bother you but I don't know anyone else. You must come with me."

Roberto nodded yes. He seemed willing to help.

"I can come with you tomorrow but it must be before work," he said.

158

Despite the nurse's request to let Giorgio sleep I felt a sudden urge to get back to the hospital as soon as possible.

"No. Now! If he is okay then it doesn't matter if we go tomorrow. But what if there are unexpected complications? What if he needs more medical assistance tonight? We might have to help him make decisions this evening. He's probably going to be fine but can't you come right away?"

I knew I sounded frantic but this was important. Giorgio, my mysterious three-day companion and new young friend needed me. If it were my son, Sean, I'd want someone to step up and help him, to make sure he wasn't alone.

"But *mia moglie*? My wife. She expects me."

"Tell your wife you'll be home a little later. That's what you told her when we were—um—together. Give me a few minutes at the hospital."

"*Susanna*, she will ask why. I have a rule—never lie to my wife. I cannot lie to her."

My voice escalated until it was piercing the sedate lobby with an inhuman shrill sound. "You lied when we spent time in my room."

"Shh," he said. "It was different. For that, it was necessary to bend my rule. But for this, I cannot lie to my wife."

Men stink, said my mom. *And you sound as naïve as the characters played by Doris Day.*

"Roberto, tell her the truth. Tell her a guest at the hotel asked you to go to the hospital to translate for her friend who got hurt. Tell her the God damn truth."

"Okay. Okay. For you I shall tell her the truth."

24: Emma Wants A Good Man

*Momism 24: If you can't get what you want, get
something better.*

"Emma, stop. My being a father has nothing to do with
you or your relationship with your boyfriend. What do
you want?" Kevin asked. "What do you want from
me?"

    In all his years of marriage Kevin had never
been unfaithful to Susan. He needed to get away from
Emma. He wanted to sever all ties and never have to
deal with this woman again. Right now he could hardly
look at her. Perhaps being brutally blunt was the best
way to straighten out her convoluted thoughts and
erratic behavior.

    "I don't want to have an affair," he said.

    "I never said anything about an affair," Emma
said, pretending to be indignant. "I know you love
Susan. You've made that quite clear in many ways."

    "She's my soul mate," Kevin said, finishing his
sandwich in three quick bites so he could end the lunch
as soon as possible. "I repeat, what do you want from
me? Why are we here having lunch alone?"

    "I know this will surprise you but I'm jealous
that you have respect at work and a wonderful family
and that your roots are here," she said.

"You're jealous of my life," Kevin said. "This is getting more absurd every time you open your mouth. Maybe you didn't hear me. I repeat, what do you want from me and why all the questions about fatherhood?"

Emma played with her coffee cup. She looked around the restaurant as if she were thinking, stalling for time to come up with reasonable answers.

Kevin remembered one of his lectures to Emma about working hard. He decided to try that tact again.

"Remember when I told you about my obsession with work? Here's another example that illustrates the importance of being accountable for your successes. In high school, while my friends played ball, I studied in the library. I studied more so I earned higher grades. It was no surprise when I graduated with the most academic honors and…"

Emma interrupted him before he could complete his sentence.

"Are you telling me this so I can add smart genes to your list of great traits?"

"No, not at all. I told you, I fix my problems by working hard. And so should you. You don't need me or anyone else to give you advice. I'm telling you this so you will start to take responsibility for your problems and your actions. You need to work on yourself."

Kevin considered getting up and walking out of the restaurant but he worried she might follow him to his office and start a scene there so he opted to continue.

""When Susan and I became a couple it was like I won an unofficial competition against my football friends. Later she used her professional skills to make me famous. We raised our kids together. She makes me laugh. We share everything. Everything. I told her about your calls and bumping into you at the dance parties. I consider such open communication part of working at our relationship."

"Do you always talk about your wife?"

"Damn it, Emma. Why don't you listen to what I'm saying? I'm talking about your need to work on yourself and your relationship with your boyfriend, if that's what you want. Maybe you should ask Susan for advice and leave me alone."

"Susan scares me," Emma said. "She was so warm to me at your house but then she wouldn't meet with me again. In the office I get compared, you know, to her all the time. I can't do anything as well as she did and I really want to."

"She is quite formidable."

"And so are you. I think you're perfect," she said. "I mean, I'm flattered you're, you know, at lunch with me today."

Kevin was distraught. Where was Susan when he needed her? Maybe if he threw a compliment to Emma she would feel good enough to move on. Part of him questioned if she wanted to have an affair even though she denied it. Why else would she be pushing for an unrealistic friendship?

"Look Emma, you are attractive, smart and independent. I admit, when I met you, for the first time I considered having a little fun until you found your Mr. Right—something separate from my marriage."

He was on unfamiliar territory and could hardly choke out the words. He looked down at his hands, feeling guilty just having such thoughts and feeling worse now that he had said them out loud.

"I know that's why you asked me to lunch. I get it and I'm flattered. Really, I am but I can't. It's not in my DNA. It's not who I am."

He stopped talking and wished he were in Italy.

"I know there's a stereotype of men cheating but not all men wander. Almost all of my friends are faithful. And so am I."

He took a deep breath. He opened his mouth, unsure of what he was about to say next. He decided to keep it light, as if that were possible with this girl.

"Emma, I am confident you will figure out how to reach your goals and how to snag that boyfriend of yours. It's what you want, right."

Emma remained calm. She held her large coffee cup close to her mouth, stared at him, put down her coffee.

"I think you're the one who's sending out mixed messages."

"How so?" Kevin asked.

"First, you tell me not to call you but you danced with me. Then you tell me to leave you alone but you came to lunch and you agreed to help me with my boyfriend."

Kevin was astounded at how she interpreted innocent actions to suit her fantasies.

"Those aren't mixed messages. Dancing with you was polite," he said. "It's the protocol at these events. And as to advice, Susan and I are both happy to help people. And lunch—you absolutely promised to leave me alone if I shared this hour with you."

"Do you always say no when you mean yes?" she asked.

Kevin was a heart beat away from screaming.

"So you *are* trying to seduce me," he said in too loud a voice.

The heavy-set couple at the next table stared at them. Kevin was glad he didn't know them. This Panera wasn't far from his office and though not exactly in his neighborhood, it was a popular place for many of his friends.

Emma smiled. "I'm playing with you but I've also given this a lot of thought."

"Huh?" Kevin said, perplexed and anxious to get out of there as fast as he could.

"I—want—you to be the father of my child."

25: Truth Always Surfaces

Momism 25: Life trumps naked.

While Roberto talked to the nurse I paced the deserted corridor. Nobody else was around to be bothered by my heels clicking on the linoleum floor or the sound bouncing off the pristine white walls decorated with a horizontal green stripe across the middle. The absence of other families was eerie, so unlike the jam-packed hospitals in New York. Maybe with the country's National Health Service people could afford to go to private doctors for minor medical problems. Maybe only emergencies went to hospitals.

"*Susanna*, your friend has stitches on his face," Roberto said. "His wound is not deep but he will have *una grossa cicatrice*—a big scar. He can leave in the morning."

My initial relief was immediately replaced by apprehension. "They said he isn't Italian. Who is he, Roberto? Can you find out?"

"He isn't Italian! When he spoke English, his accent was unfamiliar. I couldn't place it. At the hotel I tried to have a conversation with him in Italian. That explains why he rushed away."

Roberto, the nurse and I were the only three people in the hall. If we stood together our conversation might have been easier but the nurse kept her distance. I moved closer to her. She edged away. Roberto had to walk back and forth from me to the nurse, then back to me to share bits of information.

"*Susanna*, this man, Giorgio Molenkov, was born in Belarus but he has a green card. He says he lives in the USA."

"Belarus! White Russia. My ancestors came from Belarus. Are you sure?"

Roberto didn't answer. He clutched his chest and broke out in a sweat. He was having trouble breathing.

"Nurse! Help!" I yelled.

At first I thought it was his acid reflux again. When he doubled over I feared it was more serious. The nurse took charge, belting out orders in Italian. Men appeared with a stretcher on wheels. Roberto was awake, able to speak.

"*Susanna*, I am afraid."

Medical staff sped him down the corridor toward an elevator. I ran alongside. Mom raced next to me, surprisingly fast.

"*Per favore*," Roberto said, lapsing into Italian. "*Chiama mia moglie*. Call my wife, Francesca. Her number is on my mobile phone—in my pocket. She must come right away. *Ho Paura*. I'm scared."

"My God. I was naked with you and I'm supposed to call your wife!"

For God's sake, Susan, Mom said. *Take the high road. Life trumps naked.*

The nurse took Roberto's cell phone from his pocket. He clutched his chest again. I continued to run beside the stretcher cursing my heels.

"Signora, you cannot go in," she said as the elevator doors opened. "He needs to be with the doctor."

"Can you call his wife? I don't speak Italian."

"Of course, signora. And your—nephew—wants you. He wants to see you now."

Giorgio's room was down the same corridor past the elevator. He was one of four patients, each separated by a curtain. Dressed in a hospital gown and propped up in a sitting position he looked young and vulnerable. A huge bandage covered the right side of his face.

"I see you feel better," I said, thinking of Kevin when I saw the size of the bandage. I bet Kevin could minimize whatever scar was buried beneath the bandage.

"I told the nurse I was your aunt. I thought they'd be more receptive to a relative. Just a little lie. You understand a lie."

Giorgio turned away, stared out the window as silent as if I weren't there. He reminded me of Sean as a kid when he hadn't done his homework and didn't want to lie about it.

"Sorry, kiddo. Game's up. I can walk out of here or maybe I can help you get back to Belarus." The mother in me softened when he looked at me like a lost child. "You've got five more minutes, then I'm gone."

I knew I wasn't going to abandon him like this but I also was determined to get more information.

"Please don't leave. I need your help," he said.
"It's true. I'm from Belarus but I won't go back. I live in the States. Permanently. Besides, I like you. You're not what I thought you'd be."

"What do you mean I'm not what you thought I would be? What's going on?"

"So many questions."

Painkillers made Giorgio sleepy. He closed his eyes but I continued to talk figuring he might still be listening.

"You're not a professor of Italian literature. You're not any kind of professor," I said, raising my voice, losing my composure.

"Shh," said another patient in the room.

To say I was shocked is an understatement. I had nothing to compare this to, nothing in my life, my work, even a movie or book. I couldn't discuss it with Kevin because it would hurt his feelings to know I befriended someone when I claimed to want to be alone. What a mess.

In hindsight, there were clues this man was not legit. He never spoke Italian. He didn't read the menus when he ordered our food. His accent was not as heavy as Roberto's but I thought it was because he had lived in the States. I had no idea it wasn't an Italian accent.

"Did you like *Catch 22*?" I asked turning back to the subject of books to see if he knew literature or a popular novel or if he was a phony.

"What is it?" Giorgio asked.

It was the response I dreaded.

"A book. A famous book." Then I decided to try something that appealed to the general public. "What about *The Firm*? Did you read *The Firm* or see the movie?"

"No."

"I guess you don't read much—in English or Italian. How come you read my favorite books? They aren't even on the best seller lists."

"You're right," he mumbled. "I'm not a professor."

I knew this by now but hearing it felt like a punch in the stomach and made my fears explode.

"What do you do?" I asked, not sure I'd get an honest answer.

"I'm a dance instructor."

Dance instructor. I thought of our performance at the disco, how amazing he was, the way he led with such confidence. Giorgio was not as good as a pro. He was a pro. Something inside told me he had arranged the evening because he already knew I liked to dance. It was all part of a well-orchestrated plan. But why? How would I explain my lack of good judgment of character to my husband? Maybe I shouldn't mention Giorgio—ever.

"This is some kind of weird set-up," I whispered. "Who would do that to me? I'm not a celebrity or super rich. What's going on?"

I wanted to shake him but there was a nurse outside the door and I was afraid to create a scene. For a split second, I thought about slapping him across his bandaged face but it's not who I am. A slap would have caused more damage than I am capable of inflicting. So I just stood there, my feet cemented to the floor, my body paralyzed.

"Are you a spy?" I asked. I didn't think so. I had no information about anything. It was just the first thing that came to my mind. Maybe I've read too many mysteries.

Giorgio laughed. The movement caused him pain and he moaned.

"I told you. I'm a dance instructor in the States." He tightened his lips, a lock against more information.

"You sat behind me on the plane—no coincidence. Breakfast in my hotel—you knew where to find me. It was clever of you to start off at another table. You seemed sincere and friendly."

"I am sincere and friendly. Don't worry so much. Everything will be fine."

"You wear my favorite fragrance, CK One—another God damn set-up! I smell Kevin in this fiasco."

Giorgio didn't respond. He was asleep.

26: Emma Wants A Soul Mate

Momism 26: Expect the unexpected.

Kevin watched Emma trace and retrace the rim of her paper cup with her index finger. "I don't want to go to bed with you," she said. "You stay faithful to Susan. I just need a vial of your sperm. My doctor will take care of everything else."

For the first time during lunch, Kevin was glad they were sitting at a table in the back. He almost raised his eyebrows but he couldn't because they were frozen with Botox.

For months he had thought Emma might want to have an affair. It had piqued his fantasies, tested his commitment to Susan, his moral values. But all she wanted was his sperm. Not that giving her his sperm was a minor act. He never intended to have an affair but at his age, being desired by someone so young and beautiful was even more exciting than when he was in his twenties. It took a while for him to process the rejection.

"Did you ever want to sleep with me?" he asked.

Emma shook her head. "No," she said. "And I don't want you to pay for anything, you know. I earn enough money and have enough love to take care of my baby on my own. It won't be in the same luxurious style your other children have but it will be fine. And I prefer that you leave us alone. Susan doesn't have to find out anything about this."

Kevin sat up straighter. "You're acting like it's a done deal and all you have to do is fill in the date. But let's look at reality here. What about this boyfriend of yours? Why not use his sperm?"

"My boyfriend says he wants a family but he doesn't want to have a baby right away. Maybe that's why he flew to Europe without me. Maybe we aren't the couple I think we are. If he's not so interested in me I can't wait to find Mr. Right. Every time my mother comes to New York she reminds me I don't have many fertile years left. I just want you to donate your sperm."

"Emma, I'm a devoted father. There is no way I would agree to have a child and not be involved. It would not be your baby. It would be our baby. I would never abandon it and I would never do that to Susan. Besides, I'm too old to have another kid."

He looked at her sad face and felt sorry for her. Her thinking process was off. He wanted to help clear her head and shift into a more rational point of view.

"Emma, you only think you want me to father your child. I've been listening to you over the past few months. We haven't talked often but I feel I know you a little. I think you want a traditional family, a traditional life, maybe even in Cleveland rather than New York. I believe you really want your boyfriend to marry you. This meeting is a mistake."

Emma's eyes teared up. She wiped the corners trying not to smear her makeup.

"I kind of expected you to say no."

"We'll just add this to your list of descriptions: Mistaken vixen, smart woman in search of her

Midwestern values and confused future mother. Now let's see which one wins."

"That's not funny," Emma said. "Now I'm embarrassed."

"You should be. The whole thing is stupid. You're better than this. If you love your boyfriend, you need to try to make it work. Remember the concept of work? Have you let your boyfriend know how serious you are about starting a family soon? Maybe if he understood, he'd be delighted, or at least more flexible."

Kevin sat back staring at Emma and evaluating the situation as if he were her father.

"You have to see things the way they are, not the way you want them to be. You have to start with the way something is. At least your guy is available. Talk to him. If he won't commit, even if you love him, move on. Believe me, this little piece of advice is worth more than my semen," Kevin said, while taking another sip of his coffee.

Finally, he felt better. He could help this girl and stop the nonsense that had been floating inside his head over the past few months.

"That's the problem," she said. "I don't know how available Giorgio is."

Kevin almost spit out his coffee. "Giorgio? Giorgio who?"

"Molenkov. Giorgio Molenkov."

"My patient?" Kevin asked.

"Yes. He flew to Italy without me. What kind of boyfriend is that?" She looked directly at Kevin. "I guess you know he's a professional dance instructor from Belarus but he has a Green Card. He's going to make New York his home. He's here to stay."

"Certainly I know. In addition to being my patient, once, when Susan stayed home, he was the guest instructor at one of our classes. We never worked with him as a couple and Susan never met him. He is a fabulous dancer. Did you meet at a dance party?"

"No. We met in your office—on my second visit. We stepped outside to smoke." Her mood shifted and she smiled playfully.

"I guess you could say having a nose job helped me find Mr. Right—if he is Mr. Right. He says he loves me, but how can I be sure?"

Kevin leaned back, sighed. "Did he ask you to marry him?"

"No."

"So once again you are jumping ahead. I'm afraid you'll have to trust your gut right now," he said regrouping. "Emma, I have been away from the dating scene most of my adult life. I am not sure I am the best person to give you advice. However, I do believe in the goodness of people."

He paused, deep in thought while Emma kept quiet waiting for him to continue.

"Okay, maybe I *should* be like a father to you," he said. "Let me play papa and try to solve this little dilemma. In the past three months I haven't been able to help Susan lift her depression. Maybe I can help you in a small way."

When they left Panera he walked behind her, glancing from side to side like a spectator at a tennis match. If anybody recognized him, he wanted to know about it before a gossip told his wife he had been seen with a hot young woman. Maybe he wouldn't tell Susan he had shared coffee with Emma at Panera. Then again, maybe keeping it a secret would make it worse than it was if she ever found out.

"Where are you?" Emma asked looking behind her and slowing down until they were side by side. Of course a couple in the street waved. It was Linda and

Robert Freeman, the people who lived below them in the same elevator bank. Their kids had grown up together, enjoyed play dates and shared homework.

About eight years ago Kevin performed an eye and brow lift and facial peel for Linda. She was never happy with the results. She became angry when he wouldn't enlarge her lips. Linda and Susan were cordial but their couples' friendship had dissolved. It was awkward when they saw each other in the lobby. Even the doormen knew what had happened.

"Fuck! I knew I shouldn't have come here with you," he said softly then sulked while he walked back toward his office.

"I have a plan," he said, wondering how long it would take Linda to let Susan know she had seen them. Now he'd have to tell his wife.

"You're coming to Italy with me," Kevin said. "You're going to see Giorgio."

Stunned, Emma broke out in a wide-eyed, I hit the jackpot, smile. "Dr. Kendall, she said, "I'm not sure where in Italy he is and I don't think he wants me there. I could have bought a ticket to go with him but he never asked me to come along. He said he had a job to do."

"First, I'm sure we can find him," Kevin said. "I'm meeting Susan in Venice. We'll fly over tomorrow. If you can't afford the ticket, I can help you out. More important, how fast can you pack?"

Though Emma wondered why Kevin was willing to help her pay for her flight and to have her tag along, she decided not to question it. She had been dreaming about meeting Giorgio in Italy and this was her chance, or her excuse to do what she had wanted to do anyway.

"Kevin, you are such a good friend," she said, "but I prefer to pay my own way."

"I'm not your friend. I just live by the heart, remember?" he said flailing around for a logical reason for his spontaneous invitation. Maybe he thought uniting Emma and Giorgio would remove Emma from his radar. Maybe she would leave him alone.

"Call Giorgio. Tell him you're coming to Italy and find out where he is."

Emma dialed his cell number. No answer.

"Kevin," she said. "He hasn't answered my calls in three days."

27: Wives Come First

Momism 27: Not all first wives are frumpy.

Back in the hospital, I had to face the same nurse. At first she kept away, talking to an attractive woman with shoulder-length brown hair and oversized glasses. I wanted her fire engine red A-line dress with the sexy V-neck. It fit perfectly over her ample breasts and I knew it would fit me. She looked about sixty, no plastic surgery, no Botox. Despite her age and an extra thirty pounds, the woman was seductive in a Sophia Loren way. When our eyes met, she nodded.

Simona, the nurse, came over to me to translate in her broken English. That's when I learned the lady was Roberto's wife. Why did I imagine she would be frumpy? I'm a good person with traditional moral values yet here I was, about to face the wife of a man I saw naked—in my bed. An oppressive guilty feeling engulfed me again. She was stunning. Why would he cheat on her?

"*Francesca ti ringrazia—Francesca* says *grazie* for to save her husband," the nurse said.

"Me? I didn't save him. This was a coincidence. Please tell her she doesn't need to thank me. I didn't do anything."

"*Signora, Francesca* thinks her husband was saved because his heart acted up while he was in the *ospedale*. He came here to help you and your nephew. She believes you saved his life. She wants you to come to her house for dinner. Her *figlia,* her daughter, wants to meet you—to thank you."

Ich, I thought.

"How lovely, but I can't," I said, too embarrassed to be near her. "Tell her I am relieved and glad Roberto will be fine but I can't join them for dinner. I am going to Venice today."

I lowered my head, an ostrich avoiding reality. I wanted to ask her where she bought her dress but it seemed inappropriate and I wasn't sure the nurse could understand enough to translate. I edged past them to get to Giorgio's room.

Giorgio was sitting up wearing his black shirt with the dried blood from the accident. Despite my fears, the mother in me had bought him a fresh shirt. I realized how sneaky, and maybe worse, he was. At the same time, though I can't tell you why, I also felt I had to help him. He seemed more alert than during my last visit to his room.

"Hey, kiddo, you'll be released within the hour," I said. "Last chance. Who are you? Why do you know so much about me?"

He looked dumb staring at nothing. I felt my age—in a good way. I felt stronger. No more playing with my hair. No more coy smiles.

"Should I call the police?" I asked getting right to the point. This made him straighten up.

"That's so mean," he said. "Besides, what would you tell them? I pretended to be a professor. I listened to you, made you feel good. We danced. I touched your shoulder. Nothing happened," he said. "You don't understand. I helped you."

"What are you talking about? Helped me? I don't need your help. You scare me."

Of course, Mom was right there protecting me as always.

Susan, get out of here, she said. *Now!*

"You have nothing to be afraid of. I'm just a dance instructor who made you smile. Friends?"

"Friends? I'm not your friend."

"Okay. Okay. What do you want to know about me? I grew up in Belarus. My family is there. I teach ballroom dance in New York. Some day I'll be an American citizen and have my own dance studio. All I need to do is save up another few thousand dollars. I almost have enough."

"Why didn't you tell me the truth?" I asked. "It's not a bad truth. I would have talked to you anyway."

I wondered if he had befriended me for money. Was he going to ask for a few thousand dollars? I could understand that more than I could understand him wanting to be with me for any other reason.

Giorgio looked away.

"You still haven't explained why you are here alone, following me, while you have a girlfriend in New York. And now I want to know how you knew which books I read and that I like CK One. None of this makes sense."

He took his time to answer. I waited it out, trying to live with the silence.

"I've only known my girlfriend for three months but I know she is the one for me. I want to marry her."

"So why don't you?"

He paused. By this time I was used to his stalling but was startled at his next comment. I didn't see it coming. I was blindsided.

He cleared his throat more than once. "I'm already married," he said softly.

Mom is right, I thought. *Men stink.*

"Married! You're married and dating. Does your girlfriend know?" I asked. "Does she know you are married and not available and that is why you are delaying a commitment?" I felt protective toward his girlfriend even though I didn't know her.

"Not yet. I married young. My wife won't leave her mother. She doesn't want to come to America. It's not a real marriage. Many times I asked for a divorce but she wouldn't let go. Now she is in love with someone else so it will happen. I shall be free and then I can tell my girlfriend."

"This isn't so terrible. You didn't have to be such a creep. You didn't have to lie," I said.

"A little lie. Mostly I just left out some facts."

Same thing, I thought. "A minute ago I was going to give you a clean shirt I bought and ask Kevin to fix your face. But I'm confused. I need to process this. I need to get out of here on my own. I'm going to meet Kevin in Venice this afternoon."

"Please, Susan, I know I have no right to ask, but let me come with you. I also have to meet someone in Venice. Let's travel together and separate when we get there. It would be better for both of us."

"Better? I doubt it. You knew who I was when we met on the plane, right?"

He didn't speak.

"Right?"

He looked at me then stared at the ceiling, at the white glossy wall, then back at me. By the time he was willing to respond I already figured out the answer.

"Yes, I knew who you were on the plane," he said. "Let's make a deal. Let me come with you to Venice and I'll tell you everything."

"Tell me now."

"It's too long a story. I'm tired. I'll tell you on the way to Venice."

"Not a chance," I said, and then threw the new shirt at him.

28: Emma Wants To Fly To Italy

Momism 28: Never reject yourself.

Emma called her mom in Cleveland to ask a favor.
"Mom, I'm going to Italy to meet Giorgio," she
said, while puffing on a cigarette.

"No, honey. That's not how it works," Pat
said. "Don't run after him. You'll lose all power if
you chase him."

Emma held the phone with one hand and
opened her suitcase with the other. She placed
three pairs of jeans into her bag.

Emma believed it wasn't about power. It
was about love. Her feelings were the adrenaline
driving her, pushing her, propelling her to fly to
Europe. She could almost sense her boyfriend's
muscular arms around her waist.

"Why are you always so negative? Why
can't you be happy for me? I mean, Giorgio called.
He had an accident and needs me. He *asked* me to
fly to Venice right after Dr. Kendall said he'd help
me buy a ticket. It's such a coincidence. Don't you
see, it's meant to be."

"I don't believe in coincidences," Pat said.
"Don't go. Make Giorgio come to you. And why

would your doctor want to help pay for your ticket? Are you doing something you shouldn't be doing with him?"

"I like to flirt but I am not doing anything with Dr. Kendall. I'm not sure why he offered to help pay for my ticket. It's a bit puzzling but who cares. I'm going to Italy to be with my guy."

Pat was not sure she believed her daughter but decided to hear her out.

"I want to have a stronger relationship with Giorgio," Emma said. "Actually, I want more than a relationship. I think I want to marry him. He also offered to pay for my ticket. All of it, but I had already bought one."

Pat wondered how her daughter could be so impulsive. Certainly she needed more than a few months to sort out her feelings toward this man.

"Mom, *Giorgio* called *me*," Emma said. "He told me he missed me, said his work is almost finished. He wants to be with me—only me. He doesn't want me to date anyone else. That's a good sign, right?"

Pat agreed it was a good sign but the whole ticket thing by both Dr. Kendall and Giorgio felt odd to her. Why were both men willing to shell out so much money to fly her daughter to Italy?

Emma tossed slacks into the suitcase. She folded three white tops, hugged her dog then added her jewelry and perfume to her bag.

"Can you watch Baby for me?" she asked.

"You want me to fly to New York tonight and stay in your apartment to watch your dog?"

"Yes." Emma said. "I never ask you to help me with anything. Can't you come this one time?"

"What kind of work was Giorgio doing in Italy?"

182

"I didn't ask. He wants me to join him. He wants us to be together. Isn't that enough?"

"It's enough for a trip but not for a commitment. You're too trusting."

This struck a nerve with Emma. Maybe she was too trusting. She would deal with that possibility later. Right now, she had to pack.

"Mom. Are you coming? Please come."

"If it were a baby, a grandchild, I'd come, but for a dog you insist on dressing in clothes? Why not put her in a kennel?"

"No kennel for Baby!" Emma practically shouted. "Mom, you'd be helping me figure out if I can marry Giorgio and then we'd have a baby. This is a prelude to babysitting for a real baby."

Emma knew the logic she presented was ridiculous but she didn't want to put her dog in a kennel, not even one of the upscale New York places where they read bedtime stories or offer playtime and massage to the animals.

"Mom, Giorgio is *gorgeous*. He has a perfect face, perfect body, perfect nose."

"Emma, a perfect nose has nothing to do with a relationship. It's all so shallow."

"I know, but I also feel so safe with him. He's the only dance instructor I completely trust to perform lifts. Nothing in life bothers him. He always looks at the positive side of things. When I get stressed or worried or depressed he makes me feel calm. He makes me happy, Mom."

"Is he good to you?"

"Oh, yes. He is wonderful to me. We're learning how to cook together. He wants to visit Cleveland to see where I grew up. And he wants to meet you and Daddy."

"Do you love him?" Pat asked.

"Yes," Emma said. "I love him. And he's single. Mommy, he's available."

"Then I'll come to New York to watch your dog. It will be my investment in your future but next time you bring Baby here. A real baby."

29: Art Reflects Life

Momism 29: Learn how to take care of yourself.

I had checked out of the hotel before I went to the hospital to see Giorgio. I had my bags with me and just needed to call a cab to get to the train station.

Why wasn't I surprised to see Giorgio show up on the Eurostar train to Venice much like he had appeared on the plane to Italy. Despite the bandage across his cheek he seemed to have weathered the accident so I let him lift my bag into the overhead compartment. *Might as well*, I thought. *I can hardly do it myself.*

"Did you follow me?" I asked though I believed he had.

"Yes."

"Well, at least you're being honest. I don't want you here," I said, easing into my assigned seat, avoiding eye contact like I do in the subway in New York, pretending he wasn't standing near me. He flashed his crooked smile but this time it looked like a sneer. Funny how the same trait can appear different depending on a person's mood.

He waited for a minute or two but I was determined not to chat. I refused to lift my eyes from my Kindle. The car was more than half empty so

Giorgio parked himself in the vacant seat in back of me. Kevin had bought my ticket with a reserved place before I flew to Italy. I wondered if Giorgio also had reserved his seat in advance. But how would he have known which train I would take and where I was going to sit?

The possibilities were too disturbing so I pushed all ideas out of my head. Giorgio admitted he was following me again. That must be why we were in the same part of the train. Though we didn't talk until we arrived in Venice over three hours later, I could sense his breathing behind me and I was aware of his presence.

Sometimes I smiled knowing deep inside that he had not done anything really bad. Part of me was enjoying the drama and the chase. Other times I was apprehensive, remembering he was a fraud. I knew nothing about the man who was still trailing me. I was grateful I would be with my Kevin soon.

In Venice, despite his injury, Giorgio sprang out of his seat to pull down my luggage. I let him drag both of our bags out of the station, bumping along with the wheels making a crunching sound down the exterior flight of stairs toward the Grand Canal. I thanked him with an abbreviated nod then grabbed my luggage and hired a private water taxi.

"Go away!" I said, as I stepped into the mahogany boat. I knew I didn't sound convincing. I liked him and hoped he would get plastic surgery on his beautiful face.

"Scat," I insisted as if I were shooing a stray cat out of my life though I wanted him to let me know if, in the future, he married his girlfriend. For a second, I envisioned I'd attend the wedding. Then I watched him get swallowed up by a crowd of tourists pushing onto the *vaporetto*. We were finally done. I was relieved my adventure alone was over.

On the ride to the Hotel Danieli, water from the canal sprayed onto my face much as I had imagined when I read my *Departures* magazine. *I'm here,* I thought as we approached Riva degli Schiavoni not far from the Piazza San Marco.

I sat with the driver in the front section of the taxi watching gondolas with couples or families. We passed by boats delivering food, boats removing garbage, large vaporettos and other small mahogany water taxis like the one I was in. It was as busy as any Avenue in midtown Manhattan, but far more romantic. The water from the canal lapped onto the lowest segments of buildings facing the water and forming lines of moss. We passed some well-maintained palazzos. A few had flower gardens. Others showed their age.

After registering and dropping my bags, I still had not received a text from Kevin about his arrival. I figured he was en route and I had some time to preview the Biennale Art Show. I was thrilled to have a chance to nourish my brain with a visual feast.

I had mentioned to Giorgio that I wanted to see the Sophie Calle exhibit, *Take Care of Yourself.* That's why I wasn't shocked to see him waiting in front of the French Pavilion in the *Giardini* section of the art show. Part of me was happy to see him. Part of me felt like I was being shadowed and of course, I yearned for Kevin's phone call.

"Are you still stalking me?" I asked.

"Stalking is a bit like persecuting. I am trying to spend more time with you. That's much more positive," he said.

Then his phone rang. It was the first time I noticed he received a call when we were together. He chose not to answer.

"What's this art show all about?" he asked.

"Every other year Venice hosts an art exhibition. Over 100 nations from all over the world participate. Each sends one artist and one installation to interpret a prearranged theme. It's not the kind of art you buy. It's more thought provoking," I said. "This year's theme is "Think with the Senses—Feel with the Mind: Art in the Present Tense.""

Giorgio acted as if we were a team and walked next to me into the French Pavilion. After our time together over the past few days it was easy to revert to the light, flirtatious camaraderie we had shared. Maybe I shouldn't have felt comfortable, but I did. I was having fun, though I knew I had to ditch him before I met up with Kevin.

"So this is the French exhibit," he said. "Tell me again. Who is the artist?"

"Sophie Calle. She's a conceptual artist close to my age. After several years, her younger boyfriend broke up with her via e-mail. E-mail," I said.

"Many people meet online so perhaps it makes sense to break up online," he said. "It's very modern, no?"

"I don't know how they met. Breaking up online is cold," I said, engaging in a superficial conversation though I suspected Giorgio was far more complicated and maybe more dangerous than he appeared. Then I got angry with myself for flip-flopping. I like him. He frightens me. I have to get rid of him. I want to see the exhibit with him. I want to see the exhibit with Kevin.

"There must have been a reason," Giorgio said.

"A reason for what?" I asked losing track of our conversation.

"A reason why this man broke up with the French artist," he said. "You're here but you're not really here, are you? There must have been a reason for the email. There's always a reason for everything, even if we don't see it right away."

"There was," I said. "He wanted to be with other women so he cut off the relationship. Evidently, when they first started dating, she made him promise not to seek other women while he was with her. If he did, they agreed in advance that they would part. So, in his email, he claimed he was interested in others and according to her rules, they had to break up. He also claimed he was in pain over the break up but it was necessary to be fair to her, or something like that."

"Well, that was thoughtful," Giorgio said sarcastically.

We stood in front of a video of Calle in which the artist watched her computer screen while she washed lettuce, sliced carrots, cut tomatoes. She chopped onions at the same moment she read that her boyfriend was ending their relationship. The artist's eyes watered. The letter concluded with, "Take Care of Yourself."

"Wait till you see how she took care of herself!" I said. "She sent copies of the letter to 107 professional women to interpret and analyze it."

"And?"

"And I think each woman saw something a little different, from reasoning to emotional confusion of the man who sent the letter. In life, I believe we all bring our own interpretation to events. We all see things differently. Look," I said pointing to the walls in the next room.

"You're getting philosophical again."

"Maybe a little but that's what I do. That's who I am sometimes. My Kevin loves how I think."

I was happy I said it. I liked being philosophical and didn't feel the need to explain or apologize. It felt good to accept myself. It was good just to be me.

We viewed the walls that were covered with videos and other visuals. There was the letter transformed into a crossword puzzle, another exhibit compared the times the boyfriend used the word I versus the word you. A lawyer and a Talmudic scholar and a psychiatrist analyzed the letter. A note from the artist's mother was included, as well.

A video showed a clown reading the letter out loud. Was the clown implying that the boyfriend was a coward? Giorgio and I continued to walk through the exhibit. I felt comfortable by his side, which was confusing.

"Listen to this crowd," Giorgio said. "Most are talking against the guy. But maybe he did her a favor. It seems like only the last line, *Take Care of Yourself*, is about Sophie. The rest is about him."

While Giorgio focused on the exhibit I thought I saw Kevin dart by a door. Giorgio's phone rang again. He checked the caller ID but once again he chose not to answer.

"It's crazy but I swear I saw Kevin," I said, half to myself. "We're supposed to meet later at the hotel. He would have called if he arrived early."

When I turned back, Giorgio was gone.

30: The Plot Unfolds

Momism 30: Don't be afraid of the silence.

I ran out looking for Giorgio. First I wiggled my way between clusters of tourists. Then I raced along a wide, tree-lined street toward the *vaporetto* at the *Giardini*. While I considered whether to board the waterbus or search the grounds I saw Kevin turn right onto an expansive boulevard lined with benches and taller trees. I tailed him. Why didn't he let me know he was here? Why didn't he text me when he landed?

Kevin had on his typical light blue shirt and navy blazer with jeans. He also wore sunglasses and an Indiana Jones fedora. It was odd because he never wore a hat. Maybe he thought it served as a disguise. If so, it didn't work. He looked like Kevin in a hat.

Though the early afternoon sun cast a short shadow I followed at a distance, making sure my shaded silhouette didn't enter his space. I thought about Inspector Clouseau in *The Pink Panther*. I could hear Henry Mancini's music and fought back a smile. This was not a comedy. This was my life.

Kevin strode with a purpose, a man who knew where he was going—trying to get there as fast as possible—without attracting attention by running. When he reached the end of the shaded avenue, he turned left into a residential area just beyond a bronze statue of Garibaldi and a fountain with a bit too much moss and foliage. The street led toward the *Arsenale*, Venice's former shipyard and the location of the other half of the art show. But Kevin didn't continue much beyond the first few aged apartment buildings that had shops and cafes on the ground floor.

I imagined living in this peaceful neighborhood, taking a daily stroll to the local grocer to buy a kilo of tomatoes or prosciutto and fresh bread. I glanced down a narrow side street and saw jeans, bras and sheets hanging from clotheslines strung between buildings. If I weren't in such a rush, I would have stopped to take a photo. Instead, while looking up, I tripped over a tricycle and lost my balance.

When I recovered I saw Kevin seated at an outdoor restaurant with Giorgio. Kevin still wore his hat and glasses. He still looked like Kevin. I was the Pink Panther again, ducking behind two tall potted plants at a nearby *trattoria*.

I was getting good at this trailing business. I had a clear view of Kevin and Giorgio—together. Then I understood what I had already suspected. Kevin had set me up with Giorgio. I was about to rush toward them.

Wait, my mother said. *There must be a better way to play this game.*

I hid in the alley, inching forward as close as I could without being seen. I could hear their conversation.

"Why didn't you answer my phone calls and emails? You had me worried," Kevin said.

"Christ, I was in the hospital. Can you fix my face, Doc?"

Kevin pulled off part of the bandage on Giorgio's face then patted it gently back in place. "Yes.

It looks worse than it is, but I'm afraid you'll still have a bit of a scar. Your nose is good. You like it?"

"I do. It was worth reading all those damn books. Oh my God, your cologne makes me nauseous."

Giorgio lit a cigarette. Kevin flicked away the rising smoke as it drifted toward him.

"I tried to cut out cigarettes," Giorgio said. "Impossible."

"Look, please," Kevin said, "you've got to keep our little secret."

"It's not so little and she'll figure it out, Doc. In fact, I think she figured it out when I was in the hospital. Too many coincidences. You better come up with a good Plan B."

"You're my patient so it's okay that we know each other. No problem there."

"But it's not okay that you paid me to lift her spirits and it's not okay that you thought she needed someone to protect her when she was on her own in a foreign country. She's gonna be furious."

Kevin pulled his collar. "I know she's going to be insulted. It made sense to me before she left but now it sounds so stupid. I did it because I panicked when she said she was going to Italy without me. When she lost her job, instead of building up her confidence by respecting her independence, I think I made everything worse. What can I do to make it better?"

"She'll get over it," Giorgio said. "It's odd but maybe it's not such a big deal. Lighten up. Nothing happened. Maybe she'll think it's funny, or at least a bit amusing."

"I'll just pretend she'll see some humor here," Kevin said. "But I don't really believe it."

Giorgio touched his face. "Hey doc, is there any chance you can throw in the cost of fixing my scar into our deal?"

"Sure," Kevin said with a smile. "I also tried to include the price of Emma's ticket to Italy but she is very independent and insisted on paying her own way."

Emma. Could the Emma they are talking about be the same person who took my job? I thought. *Not possible, right?*

For a brief time both men were quiet, allowing the sun to warm their faces, sipping the local wine, pushing their chairs back and stretching their legs. Perhaps they had come to the end of their discussion. Perhaps they were contemplating the better qualities of Emma's personality, her self-sufficiency and joy she was eager to share. Or perhaps each man was lost in his own vision of how this saga would play itself out.

"As long as we're renegotiating," Kevin said with a bigger smile, "Susan and I get free dance lessons—for life."

He's enjoying this, I thought. *It's one big fat joke—on me. The enabler is still clueless.*

Giorgio laughed. "For life."

"But seriously, is Susan okay? She was on the motor scooter with you. That makes me jealous. She'd never ride with me," Kevin said. "How'd you get her to jump over her shadow? I need to make sure she's really okay. I need to see her."

I softened, but not completely. The situation was too bizarre to accept. And they were enjoying themselves too much.

"She's fine. You're a lucky S.O.B. All you have to do is convince her you hired me because you love her so much."

"Any ideas?"

"Have *you* read the Italian books you gave me?"

"Hell no. I prefer non-fiction."

Keep going, Giorgio, I thought.

"Maybe you ought to pay me to teach you a few things. You might be surprised what the right kind of attention will deliver."

Kevin started to stutter so I knew he was uncomfortable. *Good,* I thought. *Let him suffer.*

"We had a deal—flirt. Watch over her. Absolutely nothing else."

Giorgio leaned back, straightened out his long legs even further under the table and glanced in my direction. I hoped he didn't see me.

"I know my Susan," Kevin said. "She wouldn't do anything. Although it's strange she never mentioned you or the accident. I wonder why she felt she had to hide you. What was she thinking?"

"Take it easy, Doc. I got my own girl, remember? She'll be here any minute so we'd better wrap up our business. If I play it right, if I can find the courage to commit, if I can convince her I am the best man for her, Emma and I will get married."

"That's a whole lot of ifs," Kevin said.

Kevin didn't know if Giorgio was the right man for Emma but he knew they both cared for one another. He wanted to help bring them together, if he could.

"I love Emma," Giorgio said. "She is my first American girlfriend who doesn't want me to change. One girl asked me to give up dance to work for her father. Another told me to go back to school to become an accountant. This one gets me. I think I can have a real American family with her. I want to belong in New York with her. I want us to make a life together and grow old together—like you and your wife, not that you are old yet. You know what I mean, right?"

Maybe Giorgio's not so bad, I thought. *Now what comes next in this soap opera?*

Kevin changed the subject. "Look, I made a mistake but you kept your side of the deal and I'll keep mine. I gave you a new nose and I'll give you enough cash to cover the first three months rent of a dance studio. Depending on the cost, you might also be able to put in a new hardwood floor and a wall of floor to ceiling mirrors. The least you can do is promise to keep our odd agreement a secret."

"Like I said, Doc, your wife will figure it out. You need a good Plan B."

I watched Giorgio punch in a number on his cell. After a split-second conversation my middle-aged woman's nightmare, Emma, came from around the corner on the other side of the restaurant. I watched her kiss both men on the cheek then sit between them. She took Giorgio's hand and it was clear she was with him.

Oh my God! It is the same Emma. My leg shook, my knees buckled and I slid to the ground. I was happy this girl was after someone other than my husband. At the same time I was incensed. All three of them were playing some sort of game while I was the only one left out. I forced myself to pull up a good memory with Kevin. I wanted to generate more positive emotions than I was feeling.

I imagined dancing with my husband in our living room. Actually, we have danced in our living room—many times. And we had sex on the floor after Sean left for college. Nobody was home. Nobody interrupted. It was one of our hottest moments. Standing in Italy, I pretended to hear the music, 'Let's Get it Started in Here' and I wanted to find a way to forgive Kevin for whatever dim-witted escapade he had arranged. I wanted to harness the power of rational thinking.

Enough, said my mother in my head. With one strong word she snapped me out of my daydream. I focused on what was going on and I stood up.

Now that I knew Emma was here for Giorgio, I realized she was the girl he had spoken about, the one he said he wants to marry. I hoped she didn't know the real reason Giorgio was in Italy without her. It would be so embarrassing.

I'm not a fighter. Not in the physical sense. But I wanted to get even for the ridiculous set-up Kevin had orchestrated. I wanted to stir things up. I dialed his cell number and watched him check caller I.D. before he answered.

"Hi, honey. Glad you called. I miss you more than ever," he said.

"Mmm. I miss you too. Where are you?" I watched him say something to Giorgio who nodded.

"Venice." He pulled his shirt collar.

I realized he was nervous because every time he gets anxious, he pulls his collar.

"Why didn't you call or answer my email?" I asked. "I knew when your plane was supposed to land but I didn't know when you would get here from the airport."

"I wanted to surprise you. I'm on the *vaporetto* on my way to Piazza San Marco near our hotel. Where are you?"

Here come the lies, I thought.

"The art show, the French exhibit."

"What's it about?"

"A couple who break up." I continued to watch him. "Why don't you drop off your luggage at the Hotel Danieli. You can unpack and freshen up and meet me for dinner at Trattoria al Gatto Nero, the famous fish restaurant I told you about before I left. It's on a little island, Burano. You'll have a fifteen-minute walk to the Fondamenta Nuove on the lagoon side where you can catch the number 12 waterbus. It takes about an hour on the boat. Tomorrow we can go to the Biennale together. I'd like to revisit the French Pavilion with you."

"I'm here now. Why do we need to wait until dinner," Kevin asked and then whispered something to Giorgio.

"It's already late in the afternoon. There's only an hour or so free and I want a little more time at the exhibits. By the way, I need your advice," I said. "I met this guy—an Italian—a professor of literature at the University of Bologna. I want to bring him home."

"You what?"

"I want to bring him home. He needs some plastic surgery on his face. He has a giant gash from a motor scooter accident."

Kevin wasn't sure how to handle this twist. Was I serious or playing with him? Either way fit my personality. He continued to hold the phone to his ear but didn't say anything.

I could see Giorgio take out his pack of Marlboros again. He offered a cigarette to Emma before taking one for himself. Then he flicked on his lighter and cupped his hand over hers as he lit first her cigarette then his own. He took a deep drag, inhaling with obvious pleasure then slowly released his breath. Kevin waved the smoke away. I was so glad I wasn't sitting with them, inhaling the poison.

Most likely Giorgio was the boyfriend Emma had mentioned in our apartment shortly after her plastic surgery. The more I thought about Emma and Giorgio, the more I recalled that each one yearned to be part of a family. Maybe they would do well together and create that bond. I hoped he told her he was married and was getting a divorce. It wasn't good to start a relationship with secrets and lies. I hoped Emma would hang in until Giorgio was truly available.

But what about the secrets and lies I had created in the few days I had been on my own in Italy? Secrets and lies are just as bad in the middle of a relationship but I wasn't sure how much I would be able to share with my husband. How does one balance truth with the hurt it might cause?

Kevin was still on the line, still not saying anything. I knew he was trying to digest my request to bring Giorgio home. He was trying to figure out what I was up to.

"Come on honey, where's your compassion?" I asked. "We live from the heart, remember?"

"I remember," Kevin said. "And you need to remember how much I love you. I can hardly wait to put my arms around you."

He sounded dramatic and artificial but I let it pass. Instead, based upon my research with the concierge at the hotel, I repeated the instructions to get to Burano.

I think Kevin was surprised I had taken charge and planned everything. I hoped he was glad.

I was still watching Kevin, Giorgio and Emma while I kept my phone to my ear. I could hear whispers in the background.

"You have to tell her the truth, my friend," Giorgio said to Kevin. "I'll go back to Susan at the Biennale now but I'm not going to acknowledge your caper for you. I am not taking any heat when she finds out what you did. "

Giorgio started to walk toward the main exhibit area. I slid behind a cypress tree and reiterated my wish to introduce the Italian professor to Kevin.

"I can't wait for you two to meet," I said. "Promise to be nice."

"Why wouldn't I be nice?" he asked. "You know I love you," Kevin said changing the subject.

"I love you toooo," I oozed.

Then he and Emma ordered espresso before they each went their separate ways.

Don't say anything until you know more, Mom said, as I rushed back to the French pavilion.

31: Susan Sees It All

Momism 31: If you have your family and health, the rest is nonsense.

Giorgio was waiting for me by the time I got back to the French pavilion. I don't know how he managed to get there so fast. He cocked his head and smiled his crooked smile like a guilty kid asking forgiveness for some harmless prank. Adorable was now annoying.

"Bathroom break," I said, feeling a need to explain my absence.

"Me too," he said.

My phone rang and I was sure it was Kevin. I was wrong. It was Roberto.

"*Susanna*, I did not have a heart attack," he said. "It was *pericardite*, a cold in the muscles around the heart."

"Thanks for telling me," I said. "I was worried. Really, I was."

Well, here was my big secret on the phone. All I could think of was truth versus trust and every possibility in between. Why was this man back in my world? What could he possibly want?

"I must thank you," he said. "You saved my life. I must see you one more time."

"No. There is no reason for us to see each other one more time," I said. "I didn't save your life and you already thanked me. Your wife thanked me too. Besides, I'm in Venice."

I thought I handled this conversation correctly and was ready to hang up.

"I know," he said. "My friends at the hotel told me you checked out. You told them where you were going. They gave me your phone number. I'm in Venice, too. I'm at the train station."

My stomach jumped into my mouth and I panicked. What should I do now? How could I get rid of him?

"You're here? Did you bring Francesca?" I asked.

"Yes. We're here to celebrate my good health," he said.

What would I tell my Kevin? At least Roberto was here as a couple.

"Francesca wants to show you her clothes," Roberto said. "Maybe you can help her find a retailer to partner with in the States."

Now I understood. This trip to Venice was about Francesca and her clothing designs. It had nothing to do with Roberto and me. They were looking for a contact in America to import and sell her dresses.

"I don't sell clothes," I said. "But I truly like her dress. If she designed it, I'd *love* to see what else she has—for myself."

Life was become interesting, I thought smiling. Everyone was playing games. I decided to play, too, but I wasn't sure I could do it with a straight face.

"Roberto, my husband is here. Why don't you and your wife join us for dinner in Burano at 7:30? Take the number 12 vaporetto from Fondamenta Nuove," I said repeating what I had told Kevin. "The number 12 leaves from the lagoon side of Venice in the Cannaregio district. The waterbus will stop at Murano and Mazzorbo then go right to Burano. The restaurant, Il Gatto Nero, is on Via Giudecca 88."

"Won't you feel awkward?" he asked.

I was surprised Roberto was sensitive to my feelings. Obviously I'd feel awkward, but I was not going to tell him. I wasn't going to let anyone know anything about my encounter with Roberto. Maybe I could erase it if I pretended it never happened.

"I don't know," I said. "Perhaps, if you behave and Francesca comes with you, we can all be civil. How about you? Will you feel awkward?

"It is most unusual. I have never shared a meal, or even a drink, with the husband of one of my, how should I say it, friendlier guests at the hotel," Roberto said. "But you are different. You helped me by getting me to a hospital just before I had pain in my chest. Francesca wants to talk to you. We will come for dinner."

"Giorgio is here too. And Giorgio's girlfriend. I am going to invite them to join us as well."

"Ah, you are very popular," he said. "Francesca will be happy." He then disconnected the phone.

I turned back to Giorgio. "Kevin is in Venice," I said. "I saw you with him. He sent you here to—to entertain me. Do I have that right?"

Giorgio tried to put his arm around me, to comfort me. Any other time on this trip, when Giorgio had put his arm around me, I cuddled into the warm nook beneath his shoulder. It had felt more protective than intimate. This time I pulled away.

"I can't say but I bet if he did, it's because he loves you."

"Excuse me?" I said.

"Look, you told me you feel sad, useless, invisible. I bet your husband would do anything to make you feel better."

"You bet or you know?"

"I can't say," he said. "But you do feel better, no?" Giorgio asked.

"I feel better, yes, because you paid attention to me. That shows how superficial I am."

"Everyone needs attention. It adds flavor to life, a zing to your stride. You put your head down and stepped away from playing the game."

When did Giorgio become an expert on love and on my relationship with my husband? His words reminded me of my mom.

"Look, I need to see Kevin alone. Since our motor scooter accident all I've thought about is Kevin. He may be having a flirtation with your girlfriend."

Giorgio shook his head and laughed.

"In your gut you know that's not true."

I rolled my eyes. "Yes, I know—his heart is pure—but maybe he needs something separate. Well, I'm going to find out. Meet us at 7:30 at Il Gatto Nero on Burano. And bring Emma. I know she's here. I saw you together. I saw you both with Kevin. Now I intend to find out everything. And if you haven't already done so, you better tell her you are married and need to get a divorce. Promise me you'll tell her."

32: The Dancer Confesses

Momism 32: The Truth hurts sometimes.

Giorgio had arranged to meet Emma at Harry's Bar to share a Peach Bellini before they caught the vaporetto to Burano. He needed some time alone to answer her unasked questions about this trip. And he had something important to discuss.

Giorgio dreaded having to tell Emma he was married. Then he decided it would be good to let her know his situation because she would finally understand why he hadn't been able to commit—yet.

On the other hand, he feared she would drop him because he had kept the truth from her. He told himself he had not lied. Well, not exactly. He just left out some details. But they were critical details that could alter their relationship as fast as he could dance the Quickstep.

At first he and Emma were caught up in the euphoric spirit of seeing each other after their brief separation. She was no longer apprehensive about his rushing to Italy without her. He was glad to be with his girl after the accident. They held hands. They kissed in public. They pressed their bodies into one another and tuned out anyone who bothered to stare at them.

"I forgot to ask you about your work in Italy," Emma said, as she took her first taste of pureed white peaches and Prosecco. She probably wouldn't have asked so soon except she knew her mother would want to know. She expected a swift, simple answer, but he stayed quiet. While Giorgio seemed to be gathering his thoughts, she let her mind wander to the history of the famous bar. Giorgio could sense her interest in her surroundings and he was glad to use any excuse to delay talking about his work.

"Many famous celebrities have been here since Giuseppe Cipriani originated it in 1931," he said. "The list is long and includes Ernest Hemingway, Arturo Toscanini, Charlie Chaplin, Alfred Hitchcock and Woody Allen. Harry's Bar was so popular, in 2001 the Italian Ministry for Cultural Affairs declared it a national landmark."

It was odd that Giorgio knew so much about the bar. In New York he never quoted details about any of the places they visited. In fact, they rarely took advantage of the museums and tourist sights.

"How do you know all this? You sound like a tour guide," Emma said. "Did you study tour books?"

"A little. It was sort of, well kind of, part of my work here," Giorgio said. "Can you keep a secret?" he asked.

"I guess. If it isn't evil."

"Promise me you won't tell Dr. Kendall or his wife."

"Uh oh," Emma said. "I have a bad feeling about this. Anyhow, I don't have that kind of friendship with either one of them."

Giorgio couldn't figure out a nice way to ease into his bizarre days in Italy, so he jumped right in.

"As far as I can tell, Susan Kendall spun into a bad funk when she lost her job. She became depressed and moody. She withdrew. Dr. Kendall was rightfully concerned. Then Susan decided to go off to Italy four days before their planned vacation. Dr. Kendall went crazy."

"How do you know this?" Emma asked. "It sounds so personal and private."

"I'll get to that in a minute," Giorgio said. "Dr. Kendall worried about Susan's sadness and her ability to take care of herself in a foreign country in her depressed state of mind. She wouldn't let him join her so he hired me instead."

Emma stopped sipping her Bellini. "He hired you. To do what?" she said. "What do you mean?"

"He hired me to do two things. First, I was to flirt with her."

Emma's mouth opened but no sounds came out. She furrowed her brow like her mother, and then tilted her head to the side, focusing completely on Giorgio. Their eyes locked and Emma braced herself for a battle. After a beat or two, when it became obvious that she wasn't going to say anything, he continued to explain.

"Nothing too sexy. I was to pretend to be a young Italian man who found her interesting and fun to be with. You know, encourage her creative personality to blossom while showing her around Florence. I studied a lot of tour books for this trip. A lot."

"But you're not Italian," Emma said. "And she's old enough to be your mother. You make this sound like it was a normal thing to do. Like it was a real good job. What was the second thing?"

"Protect her. Sort of shadow her from a distance unless she allowed me to tour with her. Make sure she was okay alone. I even tracked her on her half day tour to Lucca but she doesn't know it."

Emma was still speechless. She believed Susan was so competent. Why would Dr. Kendall think Susan needed to be protected?

"For three months, I've been wishing I could be as capable as Susan Kendall. How could she let you accompany her around Florence? How did you convince her you were Italian?"

"I pretended to be an Italian professor—of Italian literature. I had to read all the books she read in her class at NYU and I had to wear that awful CK One she loves. I was surprised that my assignment, as I have begun to call it, was a pleasure. She's a good person to hang out with."

"You mean as a boyfriend? No wonder you didn't tell me the truth about your so-called work. This is incredible. That's why I couldn't join you, right?"

"Yes," he said. "That's why you couldn't join me but I wasn't with her as a boyfriend. More important, I would have preferred to be with you. I am very happy you're here now," he said, taking her hand in his and touching her cheek with his other hand.

"I don't like what you're telling me. I am having trouble accepting this," Emma said softly. "I feel so deflated. I feel like I don't really know you. Maybe people are so complicated it isn't possible to know someone for a very long time, if ever."

Giorgio understood her dilemma and tried to change her spirits.

"Listen, I read about the main attractions in Venice," he said. "I found one that is perfect for us. There is an old saying—if a couple kisses on a gondola at sunset under the Bridge of Sighs as the bells of St. Mark's toll, that couple will be granted eternal love and bliss. Are you ready to share such a kiss with me?" he asked, with his crooked smile.

Emma realized what Giorgio was suggesting and she was elated. A minute ago she had been disheartened about their relationship. Now she was optimistic. It was hard to follow the differences. She circled her index finger around the rim of her glass, and then clutched her drink while trying to steady her emotions.

"I saw an old movie about that," she said. "It was called *A Little Romance* with Laurence Olivier and Diane Lane. We can rent it when we get back. And yes, I am willing and ready to share a kiss and all it means, if you are serious."

At least Giorgio had given her a good enough reason why she had not been invited to join him in Italy. She knew she would have a tough time explaining it to her mom, but she didn't care. Giorgio wanted to be with her in eternal bliss. As corny as it sounded, she felt the same way.

"What else would you like to know about this amazing city?" he asked.

"Actually, I want to talk about something more essential. I want to talk about our future. I wouldn't have brought it up so soon, but since you invited me to share a kiss with the hope of being granted everlasting love, I think this is a good time for us to talk reality."

Emma took a deep breath. She knew it could go either way and maybe she should wait until they had a chance to enjoy each other in Venice before she put so much pressure on him.

"Okay," he said. "Fire away. I am all ears and all yours, as the saying goes."

"I want to have children," she said.

"Me too."

"Quickly," she added.

"Me too," he said. "Once we are married."

Emma was so relieved she plunged ahead at a much faster pace.

"Whew. I thought it would be more difficult to convince you," she said. "I was prepared to give you time to mull over my wishes. I also want to be married first and have a home in or near New York City with a washer and dryer and then have a baby or two."

"I'm in. I don't even need to think about it," he said. "But the timing might be a problem."

"It doesn't have to be right now," she said. "But I need to know it is coming sooner rather than later, before I am too old to have a baby."

"I want the same things," Giorgio said. "Except I never thought about a washer and dryer."

They both paused to look around the restaurant. Perhaps they realized they were carving a memory and wanted to capture details of their surroundings.

"I want to be a stay at home Mom," she said. "Or I can work part time. If you start a dance studio, I can help you. I can teach the kids or publicize the studio but I don't want a nanny to raise our kids."

"I agree with everything you are saying," Giorgio said. "We have the same dreams. I am so happy I wish this moment could last and last and last."

Emma closed her eyes while Giorgio took his index finger and played with her mouth as it curled up in a soft, peaceful smile. He stalled as long as he could, looking at her. Then he gulped down his Bellini.

"But before you get too excited, there is one more thing I need to tell you," he said.

There was no way to soften his next sentence so he paid the bill and stood, preferring to tell her as they were walking out into the crowd of tourists, his arm around her shoulder in an effort to keep her close.

Outside he whispered to her. "Emma, this is not forever but right now, today, I am already married."

33: A Slow Boat to Burano

Momism 33: Ignore it. It becomes less important in time.

When I reached the number 12 *vaporetto* I saw Kevin on line to get on the boat. At least he had taken off the ridiculous hat. I was so glad to see him I ran full speed into his arms. Then I remembered I was angry with him and pulled away. Talk about confusion. He grabbed my hand and I let him hold it. We were silent as we inched our way aboard together, pulled by the crowd of tourists jamming the flat-decked waterbus.

Roberto and Francesca were on the boat but I wasn't prepared to sit with them or to introduce Kevin yet, so I held up a finger to let Roberto know I saw him. Roberto waved as we shuffled by, balancing ourselves on the tops of the green plastic seats to avoid tipping into another passenger's lap. I sipped a can of Coca-Cola Light while enjoying the silly little drama.

"God, I'm glad to see you," Kevin said. "Great haircut. You look happy, hon. Must have been a good couple of days. But to tell you the truth, I'm glad they are over and we're together."

Still standing, Kevin opened his arms and I snuggled right into him thinking about the motor scooter accident. I sighed, joyful to be in my safe haven. Then I considered how insulted I felt and pulled away again. We stood in the aisle for a few seconds, neither one of us speaking.

A moment later, as if it were the most normal thing to do, in calm, slow motion, I poured my Coca-Cola Light on Kevin's head. I emptied the whole can while the people closest to us gasped. Others laughed. For once, my mother was speechless.

As word of my antic rippled through the rows of passengers, conversations stopped, severed in mid sentence. The only sounds were the swish of the water on the sides of the boat and a baby crying.

I watched the soda drip over Kevin's eyes, down his nose and inside the new light blue shirt I had bought him for the trip. Kevin licked cola from his lips, blinked it off his eyelashes and stared at me.

Roberto rushed over with a fresh handkerchief. Kevin accepted the cloth and wiped his face, neck and shirt. He said nothing. *A sign of guilt,* I thought.

Mom rallied. *Don't be afraid of the silence*, she said. *Wait it out. It will all come to you.*

"I'm sorry. It was a stupid thing to do," he said. "Giorgio warned me you'd figure it out."

I stood frozen.

"Say something," he said. "Damn it. Say anything."

Now it was my turn to keep quiet. I sat down in an empty aisle seat forcing Kevin to climb clumsily over my legs if he wanted to sit next to me. I saw Roberto watching us from his seat with Francesca. I loved her charcoal gray dress.

"What happened with Emma?" I asked.

"Lunch."

"Just Lunch?"

"Just lunch."

"Her place?"

"Panera's on 86th Street.

"Not romantic. Good. What else?"

"A phone call or two. You heard the calls. I stopped them fast."

"And"

"And a dance at the 92nd Street Y."

"Just a dance?"

"Just a dance."

"How often?"

"Two different parties."

I lost my breath, held my mouth. I wasn't sure what to think.

"I never intended to do anything," he said. "She was the aggressive one. Whatever temptation she provoked is gone. Over."

Kevin tried to kiss me. My husband just told me he was carrying on an unclear something with Emma and he wanted to kiss me. Clueless, once again. *He claims his heart is pure*, I thought.

"Why is she here?" I asked though I already knew it was to be with Giorgio. I still wanted to hear more from Kevin.

"You saw us?"

"Yes, Mr. Honest. Why is she here?"

"I encouraged her to fly to Venice to be with Giorgio. He's her boyfriend."

"Did you pay for her trip?" I asked assuming my husband would feel responsible for Emma's anxiety since he had arranged Giorgio's trip. Giorgio's involvement most likely upset Emma and I figured Kevin would try to make it up to her by purchasing her ticket to Europe.

"I offered, but she is very proud and independent. She wouldn't take my help. She didn't know I had sent Giorgio to Italy when I offered."

By now my satisfaction with the cola prank had dripped away, soaked up by a new wave of gloom.

"So the offer was an added option as part of your deal with Giorgio," I said. "This is so weird I don't even know what to ask. Why don't you just spew out all the absurd details?"

"I did it because I love you," he said remembering Giorgio's advice.

"Did what?" I said in a loud voice. Passengers stared at us again. I hoped most of them didn't understand English.

"What *exactly* did you do?" I repeated in a whisper.

"I hired him to flirt with you, to make you feel better. I want my old Susan back. And I wanted to make sure you were safe in a foreign country all by yourself. I know," he said, looking down. "It was a bad decision. I'm so sorry I upset you. Tell me what you want and I'll make it happen. I want to make it up to you."

"Bad decision! You *hired* a young man to befriend me in Italy. You *paid* someone to *flirt* with me. Are you crazy?" I asked wrapping my arms around myself. "You have no faith in me as an independent person. After all these years I feel like you don't know me and for sure, I don't know you."

He was quiet.

"It worked, didn't it?" he said, still looking down. "It might have been stupid on my part but you seem to have had a good time."

"You told him which books to read and he read them. That is so disturbing," I said. "Where did you get this idea?"

"A long time ago, when adultery influenced divorce payments, a patient told me he hired someone to seduce his wife. She didn't have an affair so he ended up paying a lot in alimony. I changed the goal. No affair. Just a flirtation and a guardian angel."

To say I was stunned is only half of what I felt.

"The patient was pure evil," I said. "What you did was stupid. Insulting and stupid. Showing no confidence in me and stupid. Mean and stupid. Stupid, stupid, stupid."

Kevin was silent.

I could hear my mom telling me to let it go but I was too angry to stop.

"You made Giorgio wear CK One. Do you think I'd talk to someone just because he *smells* like you? Well, right now, you stink."

More silence.

"You hired Giorgio because you have no faith in me. You know we were on the motor scooter together. When we hit the ground do you know *I* took care of *him*? And I took care of myself but all I wanted was to be in *your* arms."

It was the truth. The minute I blurted it out I felt relieved but I wasn't going to let Kevin off so easily.

Kevin opened his mouth but said nothing. He just sat there looking perplexed. I wanted a reaction, something other than his silence. Then I didn't like what he said.

"You never mentioned Giorgio in any of your emails," he said. "What was going on inside your head?

Guilty as accused, I thought.

"Can you imagine what I was thinking? You go off in a huff by yourself to Florence to be alone and I *know* you're not alone but you don't say a word."

Now I was silent. Roberto broke the deadlock.

"That guy who gave me the handkerchief seems to know you," Kevin said, pointing to Roberto who was waving to get my attention.

I turned toward him, smiled then turned back toward Kevin.

"It's Roberto," I said, still smiling.

"Roberto? Who's Roberto?"

"Someone I met. On my own," I said giggling. My moods were extreme but so was the situation.

Kevin pulled his collar. It was a sign I was on top and I relished it.

"I must talk to him. Wait here," I said, then practically floated to the back of the boat, one foot deliberately placed in front of the other in slow motion. Roberto followed. I nodded to Francesca. She waved but made no effort to join us. *There is a woman with confidence,* I thought.

Roberto kissed me on both cheeks. It meant nothing. It's just the Italian way, like shaking hands in America.

After a brief hello, I blurted out, "Kev hired Giorgio to *be* with me." The words gushed out. I was slightly out of control.

"I don't understand. Is this another American thing?" Roberto asked.

Of course he didn't understand. Neither did I. And why was I telling him more private details about my life? I couldn't stop. I probably would have told anyone on the boat who would listen to me.

"I was such an easy target—for Giorgio—and for you," I said. "So hungry for attention. Maybe Kevin and I should go for counseling."

Mom spoke up sharply, in staccato. *No! No shrink,* she yelled. *A shrink will blame everything on your mother.*

"I don't understand. Nothing happened," Roberto said.

My head moved like a spectator at a tennis match seeing myself with Roberto in back of the boat, and then looking at Kevin sitting in the middle of the enclosed area.

"Nothing happened? My husband hired a young man to pick me up. He *hired* someone to flirt with me. And I *liked* it. It worked. I felt better."

I thought about what I was saying. "Maybe I should *thank* Kevin."

"I'm attracted to you," Roberto said, "and nobody hired me. In Italy, if you want things to stay the same we know *e' molto meglio stare tranquilli*—it is best to keep quiet. Let him have his secret with Giorgio."

"It's too late. He knows I know. He already apologized."

I could see Kevin's eyes on us. I hoped he was worried.

"Besides, I'm not so sure I want everything to stay the same."

"Remember your light, *Susanna*," Roberto said, jumping into his psychobabble mode. "And come say hello to Francesca. She is anxious to talk to you."

"Later," I said. "We have time and I want to get back to Kevin. Please don't say anything to my husband about that night in the hotel."

"Like I said, In Italy, if you want things to stay the same *e' molto meglio stare tranquilli*—it is best to keep quiet."

Roberto gave the same dramatic bow he gave me in my upgraded junior suite in the Westin Excelsior. It made me think of him limp. I watched him walk back to Francesca who smiled as if watching her husband talk to another woman in private was the most natural, pleasant event for her to witness. *Now that's strength*, I thought, *or is it a bit foolish?*

I returned to Kevin and rested my head on his shoulder. I was drained and not sure what to do next.

34: Think Ahead

Momism 34: Mothers' fears are never done.

I closed my eyes and Mom popped up. I knew it was
going to be a long, hard conversation but that was okay.
I needed her input. But this time Mom was off the
mark. She feared I would go to the extreme and leave
Kevin. I wasn't used to her being so far out of touch
with my reality.

Okay, maybe, for less than half a second, I
wondered if a break would be right for Kevin and me.
Not a permanent break. Rather, a more than four day
break. Maybe that's why I imagined Mom saying things
irrelevant to the situation. Maybe she was playing my
alter ego.

Susan, she said, *if you leave Kevin for another
man in two, maybe three years, you'd have the same
insecurity and control issues with a new man.*

I chewed on my mother's thoughts, wondering
if after all these years, a crack was about to break the
hold my mother had on me. *About time,* I thought.

*Mother! There is no other man. This is just
about me.*

Just think, my mother continued. *If you leave
Kevin, you leave his credit card.*

This shocked me. I have my own credit card.

218

Don't you ever listen? I'm not leaving. And that is the shallowest advice you've ever offered. Besides, I have my own credit card. I had a job, remember?

You'll get to read lots of books, Mom said.

I could envision myself in Starbuck's reading a book while eating a sandwich—alone. No big deal. I already read quite often.

You'll find somebody else to dance with, Mom said softly.

I pictured myself on a Crystal Cruise just like the one Kevin and I took to South America the year we climbed Machu Picchu. This time, I imagined myself sitting on the side of the room with a group of single older women waiting to dance with the men hired to be their partners.

Don't worry about Kevin, Mom said. *He'll find someone else.*

I wanted to ignore her messages but they pounded in my head carrying powerful possibilities. I could envision Kevin bringing a beautiful date, maybe even younger than Jenny, to dinner at Jenny's apartment. My imagination was so damn stereotypical.

You'll find someone else, Mom added. *And then your next husband,* my mother said, *might have his own children.*

This time I saw myself at a restaurant, perhaps Nicola's on East 84th Street not far from our apartment. We'd be at a cozy table in the back. My date's grown daughter would arrive late and ask me to move over so she could sit next to her dad.

Maybe what you have is good enough, my mom said, changing her strategy. I knew she'd say whatever she thought would make me stay with Kevin. But I had no intention of leaving him. Ever. I love him.

Mom, cut it out. Good enough is never enough. I love my husband.

I'm glad because at your age, she said, *you'll never find another Kevin.*

This isn't about my marriage. This is about finding myself.

Finding yourself? That's for college kids. It's too late for you. Be happy the way you are.

I watched an old man zip up his wife's jacket and brush back a strand of her white hair. He kissed her on the cheek and I yearned to reenact the scene with Kevin.

You're wrong. You don't have all the answers, I envisioned saying to my mother. It felt good. *And stop micro managing me. I can't always live your way.*

"What are you mumbling?" Kevin asked.

I didn't tell him about my imaginary conversation with my mother or that finally, in my mid-fifties, I wasn't taking her word as the definitive way. Would my Jen do the same to me some day? Was I already micro managing her?

"I invited Roberto to lunch with us," I said. "Giorgio, too."

"Jesus, Susan, next thing I know you'll want a group hug."

He kissed me gently, amused at the dynamics of the upcoming meal. I remembered how much he always enjoyed whatever spontaneous events I cooked up. I could see he was happy to share whatever came along.

I sensed a new beginning slinking in, the start of a better time like when we finished the car-pooling years and entered the travel years. Still, he must have been uncertain because he couldn't resist asking me, "What happened with this Roberto guy?"

I smiled. "Some psychobabble. Advice on how to live."

"Anything new?"

"He thinks we should sing in the shower."

"Dinner?"

"No dinner."

"Telephone talk?"

"No telephone talk."

"So why is he here?"

"He translated for me at the hospital. He thought he had a heart attack and his wife thinks I saved his life and I love her clothes."

"Slow down Susan. There's too much to absorb so fast. And I sense there are some unspoken parts in between," Kevin said. "I guess that trumps my lunch with Emma."

I smiled again. "This isn't a competition."

It was not a normal phrase for me to use and it prompted Kevin to look hard into my eyes, perhaps searching for some more information. I played the game, forcing him to make do with another smile. I didn't lie. I didn't cheat. I just left out a fact or two.

The *vaporetto* stopped at Murano where the glass factories flourish. Moms with strollers, tourists with luggage and many others pushed off the boat just before the next wave of passengers shoved their way on in double speed, knowing the water bus would not wait more than a minute or two.

I spotted Giorgio with Emma. It was the first time I saw them since I had spied on them at the restaurant near the Biennale. They rushed on to the boat. They were not holding hands. The smile in Giorgio's eyes was gone. Emma's mouth was drawn in a tight line. Something was wrong.

You can imagine my surprise when she left Giorgio's side and marched up to me with the determination of a pirate ready to push his prey off the edge of a plank.

"I need to talk to you," Emma said. "Alone."

35: Love Him in Spite of his Faults

Momism 35: Nobody will love you like I love you.

Giorgio winked at me but there was no joy. I turned my head and Kevin winked at me. So did Roberto. It was like a synchronized water ballet with me in the center and I wasn't sure if I were drowning or the star of the show, or if once again, it was my damn imagination.

I didn't have to respond. I didn't have to walk with Emma to find privacy in the outside front section of the boat, but I did. Neither one of us minded a sprinkle of water splashing us as the *vaporetto* chugged on the open water toward Burano. She maneuvered herself so I could lean against the only vacant spot along the railing while she balanced on her own. She seemed respectful rather than like an enemy.

"Thanks for joining me," she said. "I guess you don't like me. I don't blame you. My outburst in your apartment was a bit much and I am sorry. I am determined to do better. I don't think it will be so hard now that I am with Giorgio, if I am with Giorgio. We have a problem. A big one."

I nodded yes and waited for her to tell me that he had told her the truth about his marital status.

"Before I learned about this problem I wanted to talk to you anyway," she said. "What I really wanted to

222

ask, what I THINK I want to know, is what happened between you and Giorgio?"

"Lunch," I said.

"Just lunch?"

Suddenly I realized Emma was jealous of me.

"And dinner and dancing and a motor scooter accident," I said in a singsong sort of voice that didn't fit my age. The expression on her face showed she wasn't expecting my answer. Her mouth stayed open a beat too long. Her eyes watered. I felt like a mean girl and was sorry. I'm not a bully and I couldn't keep up the bluster. *This is silly,* I thought. *It's time to grow up.*

"Look, nothing happened. I'm old enough to be his mother. You have no reason to be jealous. I'm not a cougar and I'm not a threat."

"You underestimate your appeal," she said.

Now I liked her. Okay, I'm still a bit shallow but I don't believe I'm the only one who has mourned her younger self. How many other women have looked at recent photos and asked, are these chins all mine? Are those my thighs? How can I hide my crooked arthritic fingers? Regardless, it was time to put Giorgio's young girlfriend at ease.

"Emma, he was like a friendly puppy keeping me company," I said. "He got me to talk about my feelings. That helped me sort out some things that were bothering me. I managed to get him to talk about his life, too."

My thoughts swung from one extreme to another. Maybe my one-time enemy and I could be friendly, despite a gap of twenty years or so. I wanted to say something nice, something encouraging.

"Don't you know he was paid to spend time with me? He was not really interested. It was a job—a bizarre job, but still a job."

Emma nodded, so I knew Giorgio had told her everything about our few days together. Did he also tell her he was married? Was that the true cause of her distress?

"And you underestimate your appeal," I said. "You don't have to try so hard. You're sexy without baring your midriff."

"Giorgio likes the way I dress," she said, without sounding defensive. "It's okay, Mrs. Kendall. I know we're different. I just wish I could have some of your confidence. I could really use a whole lot of confidence right now."

"Don't believe everything you see. My confidence is sometimes an illusion," I said. "Giorgio talked about you all the time. Your energy inspires him and he knows he can keep you calm. He raved about your healthy cooking—on the rare times you didn't order in, and he craves your cookies."

Emma blushed. She looked sweet. What had I been so afraid of?

"Giorgio's in love and wants to start a family with you. I'm sure it's just a matter of time before Kevin and I will dance at your wedding."

"Oh, Mrs. Kendall, I hope you're right. I'm sorry for you that he pretended to be a professor but I'm glad he didn't go to Italy just to have a vacation without me. And Kevin, I mean Dr. Kendall," Emma said, "was always a proper gentleman."

"I'm sure," I said, not letting on how worried I had been.

"Can you give me advice?" she asked. "I bet you know what it's about."

"I thought you didn't like your job," I said.

"Not about work. I plan to quit. I want out of the corporate world. If we get married, Giorgio and I will start a dance studio together. I'll work there part of the time. I want to be able to take off to enjoy a lunch with my friends once in a while and not feel so frazzled, always looking at my watch and hurrying back to the office. We want a baby and we don't want a full-time nanny to raise our kids."

The boat jostled and Emma fell into me. We each jumped back. I held onto the rail and stayed quiet. We both knew she had much more to talk about so I waited.

"I want relationship advice," she said hanging on to a section of the handrail. "I know Giorgio told you he is married. I was stunned to hear he isn't available. I can't believe, once again, I am with someone who says he was planning to get a divorce before he met me. He says the split is not my fault and he won't go back to his wife or to Belarus."

Emma looked down while wiping a tear trickling down her cheek.

"I don't know how I can tell my mother. She agreed to watch my dog because she thinks I finally connected with someone who is available. How do I know he won't go back to his wife? That's happened to me before and I promised myself no more married men. Never again."

"There is no way to know for sure what will happen next," I said. It was a safe, rather than profound statement of the obvious. "You just have to have faith in the connection you have with Giorgio."

"My mother will be so disappointed in me—but this time I had no idea. I must have some strange DNA propelling me toward men who are unobtainable. Maybe I don't really want to connect. Maybe I am so afraid of being rejected that I like being able to blame the man's wife if our relationship ends."

I agreed that these were all possibilities but didn't say so out loud. I didn't know her well enough to play psychiatrist and I didn't want to hurt her feelings. I also believed Giorgio was genuine in his feelings toward Emma—though I didn't know for sure. How could I? I didn't want to take responsibility for the outcome of this relationship.

"In my gut I sense you are the one for him. I bet you feel it, too. You have to think with your heart and at least give it a chance," I said, remembering the theme of the Biennale.

"I haven't talked to him since he told me," Emma said. "I was so shocked I didn't cry or get angry out loud. I got quiet and withdrew. Giorgio wanted to talk but I couldn't say anything. I didn't want to listen to his excuses for being secretive. Then we stopped in Murano. He bought me a ring. It's made out of Venetian glass. He's calling it a promise ring."

"What is he promising?"

"He says once his divorce comes through he is going to buy me a diamond ring and get down on one knee and ask me to marry him."

"That's exactly what you want, right?"

"Yes," Emma said. "But how can I be sure?

I decided to take a leap and verbalize Emma's choices.

"Emma, you have a few options here. You can break up with Giorgio because he didn't tell you the whole truth and you don't trust him," I said. "You can decide not to see Giorgio until his divorce is final—or you can see him while he is in the process of making his split legal and use the time to get to know each other better. Only you know which option you will follow."

Okay," Emma said slowly, deep in thought. "I want to stay with Giorgio. That's where your advice comes in. I want you to tell me how you would do it. Tell me how can I keep my connection with Giorgio alive. Like you and Kevin. Nobody talks that.

I considered what she just said and felt good. After all, Kevin and I did have a strong connection on many levels even after so many years and so many changes in our lives. I knew in my heart we would weather whatever it was I was going through as well as the absolute nonsense he had devised for my trip.

I wondered if all married people have fantasies from time to time. Maybe those who don't act on them are the lucky ones. Maybe that's what Kevin means when he says we have to work on our relationship. I don't know. I don't have a secret system or plan and I didn't know what to say to Emma.

"I'm afraid I don't have any answers," I said. "How about some psychobabble—like singing in the shower."

She didn't find that as amusing as I did. I guess it sounded more plausible coming from Roberto with his thick Italian accent while I was stepping out of the reality of my life.

"No, really," she said. "What happens when things don't work out the way you want?"

"My mother always told me, life is an attitude," I said. "If you can't change something, change your attitude."

Neither one of us was sure if the saying fit but we both liked the idea of hanging onto something philosophical.

"So I should keep a positive attitude about the time Giorgio and I have to wait for his divorce. It forces us not to rush into marriage until we are sure we are ready. Is that what you mean?"

I nodded. Mom was there smiling, clutching her handbag with one hand and giving a thumb's up with the other. It took about another fifteen minutes to reach Burano.

36: The Designer Digs In

Momism 36: Answers come in time.

As we approached Burano, I had second thoughts about having invited Roberto and his wife to join us for dinner. This would be the first time Kevin and I would be together since I had flown to Italy and the first time we socialized with Giorgio and Emma. The dynamics were already complicated without adding another couple and this was not just any couple.

To tell you the truth, I was not comfortable about being with Kevin and Roberto. I knew Roberto wouldn't say anything to embarrass me or hurt his wife. I wasn't so sure I could keep my secret from my husband who knew me so well. He often could read my thoughts and sometimes finish my sentences. When I had asked Roberto to dinner I was angry and wanted to lash out at Kevin. I was calmer now and regretted my impulsive invitation.

Roberto brought Francesca over to Kevin and me and asked us if Francesca could speak with me. Why not? Every other variation of friendship was taking its turn among the six of us. Francesca motioned toward an empty spot near the front of the boat. Roberto tagged along to translate.

"Francesca is delighted you like her designs," he said. "As I told you on the phone, she wants to sell her dresses in America. She hopes you will bring a few home with you to show to some stores—small stores that might be willing to take two or three to start on consignment."

I had dismissed the idea the first time Roberto mentioned it but now I found it intriguing. Was it too philosophical to give meaning to my encounter with Roberto—that some unknown force orchestrated our encounter so that Francesca and I could meet and become business partners? Ridiculous, right?

By now the boat was docking. Emma and Giorgio got off holding hands again. I felt like their mother, or maybe I should say their aunt. I was happy for them. Kevin caught up with me and I quickly filled him in on Francesca's request. He loved the concept. Then again, he loves almost everything I choose to do.

"You could start on consignment," he said. "Then rent a space and open your own boutique. You could trust what Francesca shows you on line or have a wonderful excuse to fly over to Italy once or twice a year. I'd be glad to invest in your new project."

So now I am not sure if I want to explore the possibility of importing and selling Italian clothes designed by Francesca or if I am thinking of rejecting the offer because it involves Roberto—or maybe even because Kevin is warming up to it a little too much.

You are too old to be so juvenile, my mother said. *Be glad your husband is so supportive. It's a new career and you would be your own boss.*

I decided to let it sit in my subconscious. The answer will come in time. First, I need to get through this dinner.

37: Dance Me Younger

Momism 37: Dance me younger too.

As I said earlier, my perfect nose job and I sit on the patio outside La Trattoria al Gatto Nero in Burano. We are surrounded by low houses rinsed in shades of rose, blue, ochre and lime, a colorful way for fishermen to find their way home in the fog. The array of tints make this island in the Venetian Lagoon seem suspended from reality, which is a good thing, because I am not alone. For the first time in my 30-year marriage—for the first time—I picked up a man—or at least I thought I had.

My silk blouse is open one button too many allowing the lace from my black La Perla bra to peek out. *Alibi*, by Joseph Kanon, is on the table next to a pack of Marlboros. Giorgio is opposite me; his black leather jacket sits on back of his chair.

Emma is sitting next to Giorgio. She thinks we can't see her playing with him under the table while he struggles to refrain from revealing any expression. I am glad they are talking again. She keeps flashing her new Murano glass ring he bought her. She is calling it a promise ring and letting everyone know Giorgio plans to replace it with a diamond ring. My fingers are crossed on this one. I would place a bet it will happen.

Francesca is seated on the other side of Giorgio, facing her husband who is sitting on my left. Had I not known from experience that Roberto is a player, I would swear he is the most devoted husband at the table and perhaps in Burano and maybe even all of Italy. It sounds contradictory but I think his devotion to his wife is real.

Francesca hands me a package. It is a copy of the V-neck red dress she wore at the hospital. I go to the rest room to slip it on. It fits perfectly and matches my fire engine red shoes. Kevin is glad it conceals my bra and that I am smiling.

Thanks to Giorgio, or was it Roberto, or maybe even Francesca, in three nights and four days I've found my cheery button. Maybe I just have myself to thank. It's weird how a new environment can make things happen. My world as I knew it got shook up. Then I shook it up some more, but I am still the same person. I still like my life to be organized so I've decided to make a grand new plan.

Kevin said he will read my favorite books and vowed to stop trying to fix everything. He's giving lip service to all the changes he'll make. Me too and that's okay. Lip service is a start.

I know the plan for Giorgio and Emma and I believe Kevin and I will be just fine, but I still have no idea what will happen between Francesca and me. Do I want to get involved in fashion as a business? With Roberto's wife?

I'd have to learn about importing goods. I'd have to query boutiques that sell similar but not the same dresses. Maybe having our own store is the way to go. It's different from what I have done in the past but I am fascinated by the complications involved.

Dinner was civil. Each person observed the unspoken rule of not revealing secrets, though each of us knew everything. Well, almost everything.

At the end of our meal, I heard a saxophonist. He reminded me of the street musician outside my office in New York City. Since I had invited everyone, I paid the bill and we all drifted toward the music.

Giorgio grabbed Emma and they danced. When he raised her above his shoulders and she then wrapped her legs around his torso the tourists, the natives, the diners, everyone nearby seemed to inhale in one unified breath. Me too. I could never attempt those lifts. Her spins appeared effortless.

If I had not taken dance lessons, I would have thought their movements were easy. How could a few minutes on the phone with my Kevin compete with hour upon hour of Emma dancing together with Giorgio? Their attitude was all their own.

Francesca was tapping her foot, moving her shoulders. Giorgio came over and took her hand. He placed his other hand on her upper back then guided her movements in time to the music. She was a fast learner or maybe he used his professional skills to keep it simple.

Emma glided toward Roberto. I saw him give his dramatic bow then let her lead him in a dance. Other tourists soon joined them.

I grabbed Kevin's hand and pulled him toward the ferry. Or did he pull me? Either way, we were a team again racing back to our life before early retirement.

Epilogue

It is a year later. Giorgio and Emma are married. I figured they would have their wedding in Cleveland but they opted for a small ceremony in New York City. They tied their wedding bands to Baby's collar so Emma's dog could participate as the ring bearer. I won't tell you what I thought about that.

Giorgio and Emma opened the dance studio he always dreamed about. Emma is in charge of marketing. Unless Kevin and I need to attend a charity event, we take our free lesson every Thursday evening. It is our sacred date night.

They got their baby. It has one of their original noses. Grandma Pat is thrilled and claims the baby looks like her.

Francesca is flying to New York for the opening of our boutique on Madison Avenue. It is called *Susanna*'s and features clothes by—you guessed it—Italian designer, Francesca. The garments have a little extra room on top and in the hips. Colors range from black to gray to brown to blue. Blouses are white or shades of beige. Of course, Francesca's original fire engine red dress will be on display in the window. I am so excited to have this new career and to work with such a strong woman who has become a good friend.

I assume Roberto continues to try to pick up attractive, middle-aged women in the Westin Excelsior Hotel dining room. If one spills her coffee, for sure he gives her a fresh handkerchief. Sometimes I bet he dispenses psychobabble. Other times, he probably gets lucky. It is something I never discuss with anyone. Whenever I am with Francesca, I can't understand why he does this.

Jenny made a photo album of my trip to Italy. She included all the shots I had emailed to her and others she found on the Internet or in travel magazines.

She and Adam had a destination wedding at Artimino. Kevin and I walked her down the aisle. It was my Kevin's first time in Artimino and he found it as breathtaking as I did. Later we waltzed like pros.

Some guests stayed in the apartments or hotel rooms on the grounds. Others stayed in Florence about 40 minutes away. We hired vans and taxis to bring them up to the Villa. No motor scooters were permitted.

The memory of my mom was bittersweet at the wedding. I imagined her drinking Macallan 12 on the rocks, flicking her hair, sticking out her chest and smiling at the elderly single men. They didn't respond since she now exists only in my head.

As to taking care of myself, I'm confident my perfect nose job and I will come up with new rules this year. Emma and I have become friends. We meet periodically at Starbuck's over on East 86th Street. I order decaf. She prefers herbal tea. Sometimes she lets me email her mom, Pat, to give her an update on our activities.

Jenny thinks it's odd that Emma and I have helped each other get off antidepressants. I hope my daughter is not jealous of this relationship. If there is one thing I've learned as I get older, it is that there is always room for new friendships without displacing the ones we already have. Emma and I each drew up a dream list. We'll do it again next year and the year after and as many years as necessary to keep our lives washed in color and show our men how to find their way home in the fog.

Acknowledgments

This book evolved under the instruction of:
Annette Handley-Chandler, Jules Feiffer, Ursula Hegi,
Roger Rosenblatt and John Westermann.

Special thanks to:
Martin Aronson for his input on the story line.

Odette Heideman, editor of *Epiphany* literary journal,
for her helpful comments. This book would not exist
without her. She is amazing.

Kathleen Lynch of Black Kat Design for her talent and
knowledge of book production. I am so lucky to have
met her.

Steven Gottlieb, my nephew who worked at United
Talent Agency and Paradigm Agency, for his insights
into his generation and useful details concerning the
Upper East Side neighborhoods and NYC real estate.

Dr. Alan Matarasso for his input concerning the most
up-to-date plastic surgery procedures.

Dr. Elliott Weiss and Dr. Debra Wattenberg for sharing
their advice about the latest cosmetic skin procedures.

Yecheskiel Cohen, psychoanalyst and clinical psychologist, for sharing his professional understanding of the individual's search for self-value regardless of a person's age.

Mary Vettel, author, *This Ain't No Cowboy Movie* and *Death at the Drive-In* for her editing skills.

Janet Berg, author, *Rembrandt's Shadow*, for her enthusiastic encouragement.

JoAnne Phoenix, Veronique Louis, and all my readers in classes at Stony Brook Southampton College.

Valentina Ghioldi, Corrado Gallo and Sergio Dell'Orco for their help with the Italian translation and understanding of the culture in Tuscany.

Susanna Ciabatti for her input concerning the health system in Italy and the new public hospital in Prato.

Sherry Klein, writer for Playground Productions, for her input concerning sperm banks.

Tobey and Harvey Klein for introducing my husband and me to ballroom dancing at the 92nd Street Y (YM-YWHA) in Manhattan and to Lester Baptiste, Catering Manager of the 92nd Street Y and Edward Henkel, Associate Director of the Harkness Dance Center for their behind-the-scenes information.

Irwin and Diane Friedman, for encouraging us to join them in ballroom dance classes in Westchester. We miss Edgar, the best ballroom dance instructor we know.

Karolina Wysocka of the Ballroom Factory Dance Studio in Patchogue, NY.

Annette Handley-Chandler and Will Chandler for reading and rereading and rereading drafts of this book and the film script.

And of course, my friends and editors who took so much time to read my early drafts: Marty Aronson, Ana Daniel, Sergio Dell'Orco, Pat Follert, Diane Friedman, Neil Goldstein, Jerry Gottlieb, Suzanne Klein, Frank Levy, Joel Molinoff, Ellen Sax and Susan Stone.

How very lucky I am to have so much support from so many people. Thank-you.

Praise for *Dance me Younger*

Susan and the cast of characters in Marilyn Gottlieb's novel will keep you laughing and wanting more.
Annette Handley-Chandler, former literary agent and film producer. Currently Adjunct Professor at Stony Brook University and NYU Tisch.

"As a Psychoanalyst I am very fond of this book because it describes the eternal struggle of the individual for self-value and significance. As we get older we tend to worry about being appreciated and hope that others are still eager to be with us. The whole story is written with sensitivity and humor and is well worth reading."
Yecheskiel Cohen, Psychoanalyst and Clinical Psychologist

"Cosmetic rejuvenation with simple procedures like toxins, volumizers and lasers have become an important part of most women's everyday beauty routine. Gottlieb touches on these dermatologic beauty fixes in a fun and amusing way."
Debra J. Wattenberg, MD, Associate Professor of Dermatology, Mount Sinai Hospital, Founder NYskinRX and frequent guest on the *Today* show and the *Dr. Oz Show*.

"From reconstruction to cosmetic surgery—plastic surgery has made tremendous strides in techniques, technology and safety. The last decade has witnessed an explosion in non-surgical cosmetic medicine; lasers, fillers and injections. Gottlieb humorously weaves modern day plastic surgery trends into the fabric of her entertaining novel."

Alan Matarasso, MD, FACS, American Society of Plastic Surgeons, Vice President for Aesthetic Surgery and Private Practice

"Some women dance. Others play golf or tennis or Bridge, maybe even visit museums. Whatever you choose, chances are those who succeed in keeping good spirits laugh. A lot. Gottlieb's book pokes fun at this stage of life and provides some much-needed laughter.

Linda Goldstein, Docent, The Whitney Museum of American Art

"The fields of cosmetic dermatology and laser surgery have seen incredible innovations in the past ten years. New laser and energy based devices, fillers and botulinum injections allow us to now turn back the clock non-invasively. In her novel, Gottlieb artfully reveals how these new innovations have permeated our society and daily lives."

Elliot Weiss, MD, Cosmetic Dermatologist/Mohs Surgeon, Laser & Skin Surgery Center of New York (Southmapton and NYC), Clinical Assistant Professor of Dermatology Weil-Cornell Department of Dermatology.

Book Club Questions

1. Susan went through a crisis as an empty nester who also lost her job. What would you have done to reinvent yourself?

2. After being pushed into early retirement Susan needed to find herself again. At what age do people need to find themselves? How is it different when one is older compared to when one is younger?

3. Though Susan did not have sex with Roberto, did she cheat on her husband by bringing Roberto into her bed in Florence? How far does one go to be considered a cheater?

4. Nothing happened in this story, yet everything happened. How would you treat your husband if you discovered he hired someone to "flirt" with you? What did this action imply about his confidence in his wife and her ability to handle events that come with aging?

5. Many characters left out important facts. Do you consider such omissions lies and how does that affect how you trust someone?

6. Plastic surgery and cosmetic medical procedures have become more popular in recent years. Would you consider such procedures? How would you feel if your spouse did the same?

7. We all age. What are you doing to revitalize yourself as you get older?

8. Do you think there are any similarities in the marriages of people who have been together for many years? Is there a system or a reason their relationships work well for them?

9. When Giorgio married Emma he became an American citizen. How much of a deciding factor was that in his decision to marry her?

10. We all carry memories of our parents after they depart. What influence does your mother or father continue to have on your life though you no longer live together? What are some Momisms of your own?

Marilyn Gottlieb

Marilyn Gottlieb, who has published widely in magazines and literary journals, began her writing career as a columnist for *Dan's Papers* on Long Island, New York. President of The Crescendo Group, a full-service public relations firm, she was a VP and SVP at two multi-billion dollar international advertising agencies and was an adjunct professor at the New School University. Inducted into the YWCA's prestigious Academy of Women Achievers, she also was a member of the Board of Advertising Women of New York. She attended Skidmore College and earned an MA from New York University and an MFA in Writing and Literature from Stony Brook Southampton. Her first book was *Life with an Accent* (2013), an historical biography. The Young Adult Edition of *Life with an Accent* was published in 2016. This is Ms. Gottlieb's first novel.

Author photo courtesy of Alessandro Moggi, Prato, Italy.

Reader Invitation

Susan's mom gave her much advice. I call those gems Momisms and they are listed below. If you have any bits of advice your mom gave you, I invite you to share them and I shall post them on my blog. Email your Momisms to me along with your name and where you are from to: **Marilyn.momisms@gmail.com**

1. You are the merchandise. Display it well.
2. It's not fair, but that's how it is. Deal with it.
3. If you aren't married by the time you're 22, you're an old maid.
4. You are older. You should know better.
5. What you see is not always what you get.
6. You can do it if you try.
7. What's mine is mine and what's yours is mine too.
8. Be Nice.
9. Enough already.
10. Be careful what you ask for. You just might get it.
11. It shouldn't be this hard.
12. It's fun to flirt.
13. Lunch leads to dinner.
14. You are somebody's wife.
15. Be delightful and you will delight others.
16. If you play you will pay.
17. Let him think he's in control, then do it your way.
18. Better to dance with your vacuum.

19. Don't believe everything you hear.

20. Jewish girls don't ride motorcycles.

21. Never force anything.

22. Things happen for a reason.

23. You sound like Doris Day.

24. If you can't get what you want, get something better.

25. Life trumps naked.

26. Expect the unexpected.

27. Not all first wives are frumpy.

28. Never reject yourself.

29. Learn how to take care of yourself.

30. Don't be afraid of the silence.

31. If you have your family and health, the rest is nonsense.

32. The truth hurts sometimes.

33. Ignore it. It becomes less important in time.

34. Mothers' fears are never done.

35. Nobody will love you like I love you.

36. Answers come in time.

37. Dance me younger too.

Girl in the Wall

An excerpt from a soon to be released novel
by
Marilyn Gottlieb

The plan was simple. Francesca would design the clothes. I would import them and run the boutique. But the opening of our shop, called *Susanna's*, would not happen for some time.

I had signed a lease for two adjoining stores on Madison Avenue not far from our apartment over on Park and 80th[th]. Our next step was to break down the connecting wall to make two stores into one.

We had selected an architect and interior designer. We had obtained city permits and now a team of construction workers was ready to demolish the wood and plaster separating the two stores.

"I am so excited to move this dream forward," I said to the friends and relatives who were there. "I know it will be a huge success."

"I hope so," Francesca said in her broken English. She had flown in from her home in Florence to stay with me and Kevin for a few days. Despite her taking English classes for the past six months, she still needed a lot of practice to master the language.

Francesca wore her signature V-neck A-line red dress. It complemented her dark wavy hair and was accented by her red Sophia Loren oversized glasses. At 60, she was stunning in a full figured way.

I wore the same dress in charcoal gray. It went well with my red hair. I thought my grandmother's pearls added a touch of class. I hoped my fire engine red shoes suggested a burst of creativity simmering beneath my efficient personality.

My husband, Kevin, was on hand to take before and after photos. He was there to support me with my new project. He thought of it as a wonderful hobby so he had taken time off to document the birth of the boutique. Knowing how hard I worked on every project I tackled, there was a good chance this supposed hobby would become a long-term, profitable business.

Our newly married daughter, Jenny, was standing by. Our son, Sean, was away at medical school but that was not the only reason he wasn't there. His girlfriend, a fellow medical student, was substantially overweight. When we voiced our concern about her possible health issues, he thought we were superficial and hostile.

I was an ex ad industry executive. Combine my past work with Kevin's skill as one of the top plastic surgeons in Manhattan and you get two people with careers that thrived on creating positive images. Sean felt we had rejected his girlfriend based solely on her external appearance. It caused a rift between us.

"One, two, three," the group yelled together as the construction team got ready to make the first hit. Bam! The wall collapsed in the middle. Bam and bam again and the sides cracked open. Dust filled the air and settled on our clothes. Remnants of plaster flew all over the room then landed in piles on the floor.

Everyone became quiet. There was total silence as the construction company stopped.

I stepped close to the wall and screamed. "It's a bone! I think there's a bone in the wall. Oh my God, there are more bones."

Jenny immediately called 911. Her heart ached for the poor soul who had been stuffed inside the wall. She hoped the police could solve this mystery. She also hoped the dicey situation wouldn't hurt sales once we opened our door. My daughter warned me that her marketing skills might not be enough to control negative publicity.

Kevin kept snapping photos while we waited for the cops. Was it the skeleton of a human or an animal? A male or a female? How did it get inside the wall? Who owned or rented this store and building when it happened? It must have been quite some time ago because all that was left was the skeleton, a bit of fabric and a thin gold necklace with a tiny Jewish star.

Made in the USA
Middletown, DE
05 July 2016